Adult Sweaters
Knitting Seamless Raglan Top Down

Patternworks Catalog
www.patternworks.com

Call Janette
849-4716

Button-Up

Flowered Cables Cardigan

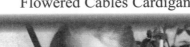

Just Peachy

Twist 'n Knit

Adult Sweaters
Knitting Seamless Raglan Top Down

Ripples Knit's Kin

Plain and Simple

Mary Rich Goodwin

Adult Sweaters–Knitting Seamless Raglan Top Down
        Step by Step Patterns and Photos
by Mary Rich Goodwin

Acknowledgments

Thank goodness for good knitting friends who are willing to lend an editing hand. A big thanks goes to Ted and Cynthia Schofield, Elizabeth J. Smith, Allyson Wray, Erin Christensen, Karla Wonacott and everyone else at Heindselman's Knit Shop who helped edit these patterns. Another thanks goes to my dear husband who unquestionably loves and accepts me and my crazy knitting whenever and wherever we go. Last, thanks to my six children who so patiently waited for mom, dinner, and the laundry while she worked on these two books.

Publisher's Cataloging-in-Publication
(Provided by Quality Books, Inc.)

Goodwin, Mary Rich.
    Adult sweaters–knitting seamless raglan top
 down : step by step patterns & photos / Mary
 Goodwin. -- 1st ed.
    p. cm.
    LCCN: 00-102562
    ISBN: 1-8881065-1-4

    1. Knitting--Patterns. 2. Sweaters.
  I. Title

TT825.G66 2000   746.43'20432
                      QBI00-443

Also available
Children's Sweaters and Hats–Knitting Seamless Raglan Top Down
        Step by Step Patterns and Photos
ISBN 1888106522 (Children) $14.95
Available from your book or craft store, or by calling Agreka Books

Cover photographs Mary Rich Goodwin
Cover design Lea Taylor

Agreka Books
800 360-5284
www.agreka.com

Table of Contents

Introduction

In 1998, I compiled my favorite patterns into a book RichDesigns One Piece Knitting, which I sold over the Internet and through craft stores. It was a success.

Now I have created eleven patterns for each of my two new books

Children Seamless Sweaters & Hats Knitting Seamless Raglan Top Down

Step by Step Patterns & Photos

Adult Sweaters Knitting Seamless Raglan Top Down

Step by Step Patterns & Photos

Of the over 2000 sweaters I have designed and knit, people say they love these beautiful sweaters the best. This book contains seamless patterns knit from the top down. With circular and double point needles, the seamless sweater is accomplished. The increases are hidden in the yoke of the sweater by working a Make 1 stitch. The texture of the yarn is important since it also helps hide the increase stitches. I call these raglan-less sweaters since there are no noticeable raglan lines down the yoke. Once the yoke is complete, the sleeves are knit circular all the way down to the cuff, using either shorter circular needles, or DP needles. The body is then knit circular on longer circular needles and there are no seams to knit together.

I explain various techniques and the reason and explanation for the different needles. I also provide helpful tips, a stitch glossary, and a design section with ideas for designing your own motifs, plus a sample of knitting graph paper for you to use.

The patterns I enjoy knitting the most are the top down seamless raglan, which I worked and changed until I had the proportions just right. It is like magic cast on so many, work the neck ribbing, divide for sleeves, front and back, and viola, a sweater. The pattern seemed to work for any size sweater knit the yoke longer and the sweater is larger.

Once you have the process down, I encourage you to use the basic sweater and try designing for yourself. Branch out and change colors, designs, add stripes or textures and create your own original sweater.

After four years teaching in the classroom, I went back to school to obtain two masters degrees in education. I began to understand even more clearly what it takes to be an effective teacher on any topic. After I published my first book, I began to learn more about writing patterns for others. Through a vast audience of knitters worldwide, I've received feedback and suggestions.

Knitting sweaters is easy for me, writing the instructions is the challenge. I've checked and re-checked these patterns, and had other knitters check and test knit them. My goal is for each pattern to be versatile enough for the knitter to pick and choose parts of the patterns and individualize them to their liking. If you come across problems, or need clarification, please contact me through email or regular mail and I will respond.

Mary Rich Goodwin
660 South 1550 East
Pleasant Grove, UT 84062
mgoodwin@utah.uswest.net

Notes on Patterns

These patterns could be referred to as "Variations on a Theme." Many of the techniques used in this book allow the patterns to be knit seamless. The goal was to make each pattern user friendly with all the information needed included with that pattern. Incorporated in these notes are some hints and tricks for making parts of knitting these sweaters easier and more professional looking. There are a few things used in most of the patterns that will be explained here and in the pattern. They are listed in the order you would need them for a knitting project, not alphabetically.

Abbreviations listed alphabetically
For more complete instructions, see stitch glossary

" --- inches
beg ---beginning
bm---beginning marker
bo----bind off
cc---contrast color
circ---circular
cn---cable needle
co--- cast on
dec---decrease
dk---double knitting weight
dp---double point needles
inc---increased
k---knit
k1inc---Knit 1 increase
k2tog---knit 2 sts together
k3tog---knit 3 sts together
lt tw---left twist
M1---Make one stitch
mc---main color
meas---measures
ndl---needle
p----purl
patt----pattern

pm---place marker
psso---pass slipped st over
rem---remaining
rep---repeat
rh---right hand
rnd---round
rs---right side
rt tw---right twist
sk---skip
sl----slip
ssk---slip, slip, knit
sm---slip marker
St st---stockinette stitch
tbl---through back loop
ws---wrong side
yb--- yarn back
yds---yards
yf---yarn forward
yo---yarn over
4 st rt cable---4 stitch right cable
4 st lt cable---4 stitch left cable
6 st rt cable---6 stitch right cable
6 st rt cable---6 stitch left cable

Yarn

Texture

The following qualities of yarn work great these sweaters; textured yarn such as tweeds, multi-color, multi-strand yarns, boucle, or nubby yarns work well. There isn't one particular kind that must be used, instead, find a yarn you like and with its imperfect color or texture, you are set to knit.

Weight

You have the freedom to choose the weight of yarn you like with just about any of these patterns. If you like a thinner weight, choose a dk (double knit), or sport weight yarn. Smaller needles such as a size 6 or smaller may need to be used with the thinner yarn. The same applies to a bulky yarn, a larger size 10 or 10 1/2 needle may be a better size for that yarn. The determining factor for these patterns is the length of the yoke. The longer you knit the yoke, the larger the sweater size. As long as you make the neck large enough, the yoke determines the size of the sweater. Knit a swatch to determine gauge and looseness of desired stitch.

Fiber Content

Knit with fibers you like. Choose wool, acrylic, cotton, blends, mix and match. Make sure the washing instructions are the same for all the yarns used. If they are all machine washable, they are interchangeable. If they have different fiber and some are washable, while others are dry clean only, you may have problems. Treat all the fibers like the most delicate one you are using. If using a non-mercerized cotton, be aware the sweater will shrink, allow for this.

Colors

Have fun with colors, mix and match, use up what you have, or buy what you want. Many of these patterns can be knit for either male or female. Change the colors to suit your individual preference. Can't decided what colors to use, look to nature for your answer. Find a picture or place you find beautiful, look at the colors that are found there and match them to yarns. Many of these sweaters were designed during the fall, consequently, fall colors show in my selection.

Amount

Each variety of yarn will contain different yardage. Grams or ounces alone can vary with yardage. Check the chart included in these notes to find the yardage needed for the size sweater to be knit and the weight of yarn to be used. Each pattern will also include total yardage needed to knit the garment. Make sure you buy enough yarn to complete your project. Nothing is more disappointing than to almost finish a sweater and run out of yarn, only to find you can't match it again.

How Much Yarn Do I Need? Yardage given for sizes toddler 2 to XXXL using Stockinette Stitch. Aran knits may use 1/3 more yardage.

Size	Chest	Bulky Yarn	Worsted Weight	Sport Weight
Toddler 2	22"	350 yds	420 yds	500 yds
Toddler 4	24"	400 yds	500 yds	600 yds
Size 5-6	26"	500 yds	600 yds	700 yds
Size 8-10	28"	650 yds	800 yds	950 yds
Size 12-14	30"	800 yds	950 yds	1100 yds
Small	32 to 34"	900 yds	1050 yds	1300 yds
Medium	36 to 38"	1000 yds	1150 yds	1400 yds
Large	40 to 42"	1100 yds	1250 yds	1600 yds
X-Large	44 to 46"	1200 yds	1450 yds	1800 yds
XX-Large	48 to 50"	1400 yds	1700 yds	2000 yds
XXX-Large	52 to 54"	1600 yds	1950 yds	2200 yds

Standard Weight Yarn Gauge

Bulky	3 1/2 sts = 1 inch	4 rows = 1 inch	Size 11 needles
Worsted	5 sts = 1 inch	7 rows = 1 inch	Size 8 needles
Sport/dk	6 sts = 1 inch	8 rows = 1 inch	Size 5 needles

Needle Conversion Chart

US	Metric
1	2.25
2	2.5
3	3
4	3.5
5	3.75
6	4
7	4.5
8	5
9	5.5
10	6
10 1/2	6.5, 7, 7.5
11	8
13	9

Gauge

Choose your yarn and needles you will be using and cast on the number of stitches you need to knit 4". If the gauge is 5 sts per inch, cast on 20 sts. Knit several rows and your piece should measure 4". If it is too large, try smaller needles, if it is too small, try larger needles. Be careful not to stretch out the sample as you measure it. You might want to purl a row to separate the different sizes of needles when you change to get the correct gauge. As a general rule, 1/2 stitch difference = 1 size. In other words, if you are supposed to get 5 sts per inch and you get 4 sts per inch, and you wanted to knit a size 34, you will end up with a size 38 since the difference is 1 stitch, since 1/2 st difference = 1 size, so 1 whole stitch = 2 sizes.

You might get your sts per inch to match but find your rows don't measure up. The sts per inch are more important than the rows since the size is determined by the length of the yoke.

Needles and Other Useful Information

Circular and double point needles are the secret to knitting this sweater completely seamless. The ribbing for these sweaters is always knit on a smaller size 16" length circular needle. I like to use a size 3 needle with the sport and dk weight yarns since it produces a nice tight ribbing. A larger size 4 can be used with the worsted weight yarn and a size 6 with the bulky weight yarns. Use what you are comfortable with, or what gives you the correct gauge.

Explanation of Needle Use

All sizes use the smaller 16" circular needles for the neck, sleeve and bottom cuff ribbing.

For 3 smaller sizes 1-2-4 It's easier to use the 16" circular needles for yoke and body. The sleeves and cuffs can be worked on dp needles.

For 3 larger sizes 6-8-10 16" circular needles are used on the yoke and 24" are exchanged after yoke sts are added. The 16" needles will be used to knit the sleeves circular leaving all other sts on longer circular needle. Double point needles can also be used for seamless sleeves.

	Bulky	Worsted	Sport
Ribbing	size 6 needle	size 3`to 5 needle	size 3 needle
Body	size 10 to 10 1/2	size 8 needle	size 6 needle

If knitting a small child's sweater, it's easier to use the smaller size 16" circular needles for the neck, yoke and body. The sleeves and cuffs can be worked on dp needles since the 16" circular needles won't stretch around the sleeves.

For larger sized sweaters, the 16" circular needles are used on the ribbing and the first several inches of the yoke. Change to the larger 24" circular needles to continue the yoke and they will also be used on the body of the sweater. The 16" needles will be used to knit the sleeves circular leaving all other sts on 24" circular needles. Double point needles, the same size as the circular needles can also be utilized for seamless sleeves.

If You Don't Have all the Size Needles You Need

Don't worry, use stitch holders to hold the sts from the body and other sleeves while you knit each sleeve circular. If you can only have one length of circular needle, use the 16" length, it's easier to scrunch sts than to stretch them.

Reading Patterns

When you follow a pattern, always read between the punctuation. Read from comma to comma, comma to period, or period to period and do what it says within that section before going on to the next. When there are parenthesis, follow the instructions within them and usually what follows will tell you how many times to follow the instructions in parenthesis.

Stickies

Stickies or Post-its are a great way to keep your place in a pattern, just stick it on where you are and move it as you progress, when the sticky is gone, get another one. It is easier than getting lost and having to rip out your knitting.

Casting On

There are many different ways to cast on for the beginning of the neck ribbing. Make sure the cast on is loose enough for the opening to stretch and pull the sweater over the head comfortably. **Thumb wrap cast on:** Wrap yarn around thumb from front to back and slip needle through loop from bottom to top, for a very loose cast on. The first row to knit is a little difficult, but is easier after the first row is worked. If you have another way to cast on, use it. The cast on can be fancy or plain depending on the desired look of the edge. If you are casting on and need a tail for part of the cast on, make sure you have at least 3 times the length of tail that you will need for the length you are casting on.

Increase Stitch
The Make one stitch

(M1) is one way to increase a stitch very unnoticeably. Place the left needle under the bar between the stitch just knit and the next one ready to be knit. Lift up the bar and place the right needle through the back of that bar. Wrap it like you would to knit and follow through with a knit stitch. See following diagram for picture instructions.

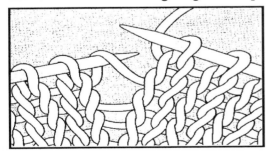 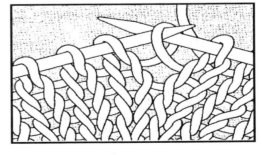

Scattering the M1's

When working the M1's, change their placement on each increase row so they don't line up. You can follow a pattern for placing them, or make them randomly and farther from the markers as more sts are added. Try to place them consistently the same number of sts from the marker for that same row. If you choose to place them 4 sts before and after the marker, work them 4 sts before and after the rest of the markers for that row.

M1's and a Fair Isle Pattern

If there is a motif such as a heart, place the M1 between the motifs so they aren't altered by the added sts. If you are designing your own pattern, place increases where they won't be noticed.

Raglanless to Raglan

If the M1 sts make you a little unsure, you can convert many of these patterns to a raglan by working a knit 1increase in the stitch before and the stitch after each marker, every other row. Knit 1increase (K1inc) is worked by knitting into the front of the stitch and in the back of the same stitch before slipping the stitch off the needle. The only difference will be a raglan line. This technique would not be suggested for the textured patterns or those with waves.

Adding Colors

When adding or changing colors, add the next color of yarn by placing at least a 6" tail of the yarn to be added behind the knitting, hold the new strand as if it were tied on. You will secure it after 1 or 2 more rows are worked so it can be adjusted and tied with no extra slack for a flawless front.

Stripeless Stripe

To knit a different color colored stripe into your sweater, there is a trick to making it a true stripe and not one with a step in it. Lay the tail of the new yarn behind the work and hold it and knit regularly without tieing it on. Tie it when you come around to that place on the next row or even after a couple of rows. When you knit around to the place where you started the next color, knit to the stitch right before the one where you added the new color. Place the right needle in the stitch below the one you would normally knit and knit it as a regular stitch. Continue knitting and repeat this same technique for the next color change.

Markers

You can purchase commercial markers, use paper clips, or rubber bands. I like to use a contrasting color of yarn for 3 of the markers and a different color for the beginning marker. Cut a 4" length of yarn and tie it in a slip knot. For the beginning marker, wrap the marker twice on the increase rows to indicate an increase row. Place beginning marker without a double wrap on regular, non increase rows. The beginning marker is usually the marker at the beginning of the sleeve section, the next marker is the beginning of the back section and the 3rd marker is the beginning of the second sleeve. If you are using commercial markers, you can also place 2 markers together at the beginning to mark this part of the garment.

Sizing

For a really good fit, find a sweater that is the size you want to knit. Measure the yoke diagonally as if it had a raglan sleeve, that measurement is a good indicator of how long you should knit the yoke for your sweater.

Note Since yarn may vary, gauge will also vary. After checking your gauge and figuring out your size, remember the length of the yoke determines the size of the sweater. Measure it from the needle to the beginning of the ribbing from a front marker, ribbing not included in the measurement. Since short rows may be worked on the back, make sure you measure it on the front side of the sweater. This measurement is the one from the base of the neck ribbing to the underarm, measured on the front section of sweater. Larger sweaters can also be made by increasing the length of the yoke from the neck to the sleeve inseam. The longer the yoke, the larger the sweater. The proportions for the front, back and sleeves will also increase to the larger size desired. 1 inch equals about 3 more inches added to chest measurement.

Ribbing

Ribbing can be changed to suit individual likings.

*K1, p1: Work continuously over an even number of sts lining up the knit sts and purl sts.

*K2, p2: Work continuously over a multiples of 4 sts. Line up the k2's and the p 2's.

*K3, p2: Worked on multiples of 5 sts. Line up the knit and purl sts.

*Rolled edge: Knit at least 6 to 8 rows of stockinette st, then work one of the previous ribbings for 1 to 2" to help pull in the neck ribbing before working the yoke. The stockinette stitch edge will roll.

Short Rows

Short rows will add 4 extra rows on the back and part of the sleeve section of the sweater for a more comfortable fit with the back of the sweater slightly longer at the neck edge. Short rows are optional on any of the patterns and can be included only if the knitter wants to add them. The short row begins on the right side of the sweater from the beginning marker.

Short Row Explanation

Two optional short rows may be knit after neck ribbing. When working short rows, 1st row will be worked from beginning marker which is the first marker of the sleeve section, across the sleeve, across the back section and other sleeve. 2nd short row is worked right after the 1st short row 2 sts beyond on both sides of the first short row.

Short Rows Directions

Slip beginning marker, knit to the fourth marker counting the beginning marker. Knit 2 more sts, yf (yarn forward), sl 1, yb (yarn back), turn work to WS (wrong side), sl 1, purl to beginning marker, purl 2 sts past beginning marker, yb, sl 1, yf, turn work, right side, sl 1, knit to where last turn was made 2 sts past the 4th marker. Knit 2 sts past this last short row turn, yf, sl 1, yb, turn work, sl 1, purl to beginning marker, purl 4 sts beyond beginning marker. Yb, sl 1, yf, turn work, sl 1, knit to beginning marker. You have just added 4 rows to the back section of the sweater for a more comfortable fit. Each pattern will take you through the short rows step by step. Remember, the short rows are optional and will not affect the overall look of the sweater.

Knitting Sleeves Flat Instead of Circular

Any of these patterns can be knit with flat sleeves instead of circular. You may not like to use double point needles, or maybe you don't know how. You will still knit over the sleeve section and leave all other sts on longer circular needles. RS, work over sleeve sts to second marker, turn work to WS, and purl back on the back side to the beg marker. Work back and forth over sleeve sts and work the decrease every 6th row except don't work the decrease on the edge of the sleeve. Work the decreases 2 or 3 sts from the edge, which will leave you a nice edge to stitch up later. For small sweaters, you can actually knit the sleeves on dp needles, only use them like straight needles. Place a rubber band or tip protector around one of the edges, so sts don't slip off. Leave about an 18" tail to stitch up seam when sweater is complete.

Sleeve Decrease

The instructions for these patterns calls for two k2togs one on each side of marker to decrease sleeve inseam. With the textured yarn, this decrease is fine for both sides of the marker since decreases are unnoticeable. If you would like to have the sts both slant into the marker, work a ssk on the right side of the marker.

Under Arm Gap

After sleeves are finished ready to be worked with the body, there will be a small gap under each arm. This can be easily knit shut on the first round when joining the front and back. As you work to the underarm, slip the left needle through a stitch from the sleeve and wrap it and knit it as normal. Pick up 1 to 2 more sts to completely close this opening. On the next round of the body, where the sts were added under each arm, work 2 k2 tog's to decrease the sts added on the previous row. The gap under the arm can always be stitched up with a tapestry needle and yarn after sweater is finished

Buttonholes

Buttonholes can be worked many different ways. The method used in these patterns is to bind off 2 to 3 sts on the button band, on the next row, cast on 2 to 3 sts where the previous sts were bound off. Buttonholes should be worked 3 or more sts from the outside edge.

10

Button Band

The button band can be knit with the rest of the sweater, or picked up after the sweater is knit and added later. To knit on the button band, here are two ways you can work it.

1. Garter Stitch Band

This is the band worked on the patterns in this book. Work a garter stitch button band on both edges of the cardigan. Knit the first 5 sts on both the knit and purl sides of fronts while knitting sweater.

2. Ribbing Edge

After working the neck ribbing, continue working the ribbing stitch down the front 6 to 8 sts on both edges of the sweater and working button holes periodically down the buttonhole edge. Make sure you work this ribbing edge tight, it has a tendancy to be loose.

Pullover to Cardigan

If a pullover is converted to a cardigan, 4 to 6 sts need to be added to front section of sweater to compensate for the button band overlap. Divide them equally between the two front sections

Length

As styles change, so do the length of sweaters, both body and sleeves. You can adjust the length of any of these patterns to suit individual body's or fashions. One advantage to knitting the top down sweater, the length can be changed easily without ripping out the whole sweater.

Binding Off

Make sure you bind off **loosely**. To help, change the right needle to a larger size, 2 to 6 sizes larger to help keep bind off stitches loose. DP needles also work well for the bind off.

Picot Edge Bind Off

For a variation on the regular bind off, try the following. Instead of wrapping the yarn over the top of the front and back when working the knit and purl stitch, use a double point needle for the right side and wrap yarn under work for the knit and purl stitch. Purl the knit sts and knit the purl sts while binding off and wrapping the yarn down under instead of over the top.

Blocking

After sweater is completed and hand work is done, lay garment flat on a table or counter and shape. Spray thoroughly with spray bottle and water until sweater is completely damp. Press each part of the garment, both front and back firmly with palms. Pounding with a flat hand may also help in pressing and shaping the sweater. Shape as desired and let dry. You may pin, or lay something with weight on edges to help hold the shape. Don't use heat or an iron on acrylic as the fibers can actually melt with heat.

Plain & Simple

And it's No Plain Jane

A stylish yet comfortable mock turtleneck tops this pullover sweater that is simple and quick to knit. Hidden increases in the yoke result in a smooth flowing effect in a top down knit raglanless look. Choose colorful and textured yarn and knit this sweater that is interesting and attractive as well.

Sizes

Sweater is written for sizes; **small, medium, large, x--large and xx-- large**. Directions are written for smallest size with larger sizes in parenthesis.

Sweater pictured was knit with Noro Oacho yarn.

Finished Chest Measurements at Underarm

Chest circumference 36 (39, 42, 45, 48)"

Materials

Yarn Nubby worsted or bulky weight total yardage needed 1050 (1150, 1250, 1450, 1700) yards.

Circular Needles One pair each size 4 and 8 16" length. One pair size 8 24" length.

Double Point Needles Size 4 and 8

Markers

Tapestry Needle

Gauge

4 sts and 6 to 7 rows = 1" working Stockinette st knit with size 8 needles. Gauge may vary with the texture of the yarn. Fewer stitches per inch will result with more nubby yarn.

Note Sweater is knit from the top down on smaller circular needles and as yoke sts increase, longer circular needles are used. Shorter needles will then be used to knit sleeves circular while all other sts remain on longer needles. If sts become too tight, dp needles can be used for remaining sleeve and cuff.

Neck Ribbing

Cast on 85 (90, 95, 100, 105) sts on size 4 16" circular needles, join with beginning to knit circular be careful not to twist stitches. Place beginning marker where sts are joined. If cast on sts are difficult to join and knit circular, turn and work the first row of ribbing, then join on the second row to knit circular.

Row 1 and all odd rows: K3, p2; rep around to beg marker.

Row 2 and all even rows: K3, p2; rep around to beg marker.

Repeat rows 1 and 2 until ribbing measures 3".

Change to larger size 8 16" circular needles.

Preparatory Row K16 (17, 19, 20, 21), place marker (sleeve); k26 (28, 28, 30, 31), place marker (back); k16 (17, 19, 20, 21), place marker (sleeve); k27 (28, 29, 30, 32), place marker (front).   Beginning marker is a different color of yarn tied in slip knot large enough to wrap around needle once or twice. Keep track of increase rows by wrapping beginning yarn marker twice, once wrapped around means no increase. You can also use 2 plastic rings for beg marker and 1 for the other 3 markers.

Optional Short Row Explanation and Directions (If you don't want to work short rows, begin with yoke directions) 4 optional short rows may be added to the back and part of the sleeve sections of sweater for a more comfortable fit. Directions are explained here and begin after the neck ribbing is finished and you have changed to larger needles. Slip beg marker (1st marker) and knit to the 4th marker. K2 sts past 4th marker, yarn forward (yf), sl 1, yarn back (yb), turn work to (WS), sl 1 st, purl to beg marker, purl 2 sts past beg marker, yb, sl 1, yf, turn work, (RS), sl 1st, knit to where last turn was made (2 sts past the 4th marker) knit 2 more sts, yf, sl 1 st, yb, turn work, (WS) sl 1 st, purl to beg marker, purl 4 sts past beg marker, yb, sl 1, yf, turn work, (RS) sl 1 st, knit to beg marker.

M1 Make 1 stitch: On knit side, with left needles, pick up the horizontal strand between last st and next st to be knit, pick it up from front to back and knit into the back of this strand with the right needle. Strand is twisted to avoid a hole. See pattern notes for detailed pictures.

Yoke

Row 1: Knit row and at same time M1 4 sts before and after each marker around to beginning marker. **Note** The M1 stitch is worked the same distance from each marker, but the number of sts changes on each inc row so they do not line up.

Row 2 and all even rows: (Don't double wrap marker for this row.) Knit row slipping markers to beg marker.

Row 3: Rep row 1 except M1 6 sts before and after each marker.

Row 5: M1 8 sts before and after each marker.

Row 7: M1 12 sts before and after each marker.

Rep this M1 pattern on odd rows changing number of sts knit before and after markers. As more sts are added to the yoke, you can work M1 st farther away from markers until the front yoke measures 11 (12, 13, 14, 15)" not including neck ribbing. Make sure you measure the front of the sweater.

Note (If you have 2 sets of needles, keep the body and other sleeve on 24 " circular needles.) With shorter 16" size 8 needles, knit over sleeve sts from the beg marker to the 2nd marker. Join the sleeve sts to knit circular. Place a marker where sleeve sts join for sleeve inseam.

Sleeves

Rows 1 to 5: Knit.

Row 6: Knit row and at same time k2tog before and after inseam marker.

Repeat this pattern of decreasing 2 sts every 6th row until sleeve inseam measures 15 (15, 16, 16, 16)". Change to smaller size 4 16" or size 4 dp needles and knit cuff ribbing. Sts may need to be decreased to have a multiple of 5 sts.

Cuff

Row 1: K3, p2; Repeat row 1 lining up knit sts and purl sts around cuff for 2". Bind off loosely.

Note When binding off, you might want to change the right needle to 2 to 6 sizes larger to help bind off loosely. Slip stitches on needles over to other sleeve section, sts between the 3rd and 4th markers. Attach yarn and with 16" size 8 needles, repeat sleeve directions.

Body

All remaining sts will be joined to knit body circular. When joining front and back sections pick up 2 to 3 sts from sleeve inseam under both sleeves on first round to close gap. With left needle, place it through an edge st from sleeve and knit it with the right needle. On next round where 2 to 3 sts were picked up, k2tog; 2 to 3 times to decrease these added sts under arm. Continue knitting body circular until it measures 13 (13, 14, 14, 15)" or desired length or the same length as the sleeves not counting the ribbing. Knit one more round and dec approx 10 sts evenly around or number to have sts that are a multiple of 5. Change to size 4 circular needles.

Bottom Ribbing

Row 1: K3, p2; repeat ribbing around to match sleeve ribbing for 2".
Bind off loosely.

Finishing

Weave in loose ends and if necessary sew gap closed under arm inseam. Block with spray mist and press with palm of hands. See detailed instructions in pattern notes for blocking.

Finished measurements of sweater

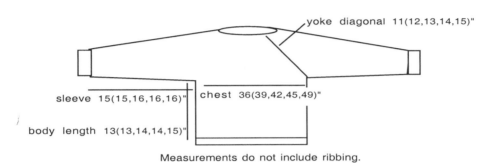

yoke diagonal 11(12,13,14,15)"

sleeve 15(15,16,16,16)"   chest 36(39,42,45,49)"

body length 13(13,14,14,15)"

Measurements do not include ribbing.

Around & About

All Around Nice and Friendly

Shetland Ragg Yarn creates a textured sweater with its two toned strand. This raglanless pullover goes solo as it is combined with contrasting colors in a fair isle stripe through the center of the sweater for a distinct expression. The yarn is the secret to this pattern as the texture adds interest to the sweater and facilitates the hidden yoke increases.

Sizes
Sweater is written for; **small, medium, large, x-large and xx-large**. Directions are written for smallest size with larger sizes in parenthesis.

Pictured sweater knit with Shetland Ragg and Canadiana.

Finished Chest Measurements at Underarm
Chest circumference 36 (39, 42, 45, 48)"

Materials
Yarn Worsted weight total yardage needed 1050 (1150, 1250, 1450, 1700) yds.
Remnants of; Gold , Black, Blue , Green , Burgundy; enough of each to work 2 to 3 rows of fair isle around body and both sleeves.
Circular Needles One pair each size 6 and 10 16" length, size 10 24" length.
Markers

16

Gauge

4 sts and 6 rows = 1" working Stockinette st knit with size 10 needles and Shetland Ragg 25% wool yarn. Gauge may vary with the texture of the yarn.

Neck Ribbing

Cast on 96 (102, 108, 114, 120) sts on size 6 16" circular needles, turn.

Rows 1 and all odd rows: K3, p3; repeat around. Join end with beginning to knit circular, be careful not to twist stitches. (By knitting this first row, joining will be easier.)

Row 2 and all even rows: K3, p3; repeat around.

Repeat row 2 for 3". Change to larger size 10 24" circular needles.

Preparatory Row: K17 (19, 20, 22, 24), place marker (sleeve); k31 (32, 34, 35, 36), place marker (back); K17 (19, 20, 22, 24), place marker (sleeve); k31 (32, 34, 35, 36), place marker, (front), Beginning marker is a different color of yarn tied in slip knot large enough to wrap around needle once or twice. **Hint**: Keep track of increase rows by wrapping yarn twice, once around means no increase.

Optional Short Row Explanation and Directions (If you don't want to work short rows, begin with yoke directions) Four optional short rows are explained here and may be knit after neck ribbing is finished and you have changed to larger needles. Slip beginning marker (1st marker) and knit to the 4th marker. K2 sts past 4th marker, yarn forward (yf), sl 1, yarn back (yb), turn work to (WS), sl 1 st, purl to beg marker, purl 2 sts past beg marker, yb, sl 1, yf, turn work, (RS), sl 1st, knit to where last turn was made (2 sts past the 4th marker) knit 2 sts past last short row turn, yf, sl 1 st, yb, turn work, (WS) sl 1 st, purl to beg marker, purl 4 sts past beg marker, yb, sl 1, yf, turn work, (RS) sl 1 st, knit to beg marker. You have just added 4 rows to the back and part of the sleeve sections of the sweater for a more comfortable fit.

M1 Make 1 stitch: On knit side, with left needles, pick up the horizontal strand between last st and next st to be knit, pick it up from front to back and knit into the back of this strand with the right needle. Strand is twisted to avoid a hole. See pattern notes for detailed picutures.

Yoke

Row 1: Knit row and at same time M1 2 sts before and after each marker.

Row 2 and all even rows: Knit row.

Row 3: M1 4 sts before and after each marker.

Row 5: M1 8 sts before and after each marker.

Row 7: M1 1 sts before and after each marker.

Row 9: M1 5 sts before and after each marker.

Row 11: M1 9 sts before and after each marker.

(The M1 st can be made farther from the marker as more sts are added.)

Rep rows 1 to 11 until yoke measures 9 (10, 11, 12, 13)" ribbing not included. Begin color chart and always start each row from the right side of the chart and at the same time continue the increase pattern every other row working the increase sts into the color pattern. There may be an extra color st where M1 is worked, overall, it won't show when the sweater is complete. When yoke measures 11 (12, 13, 14, 15)" not including the ribbing, knit to sleeve section which starts at the beg marker, you will continue with color chart

Sleeves
Sleeves will be knit while keeping all other stitches on longer circular needle. With shorter 16" size 10 circular needles, begin knitting sleeve sts from beginning marker to 2nd marker. This section will be a little narrower than the front and back sections. Join these sts to knit sleeves circular. Place a marker between beginning and end of sleeves sts to mark sleeve inseam. Continue following color chart and at same time begin underarm sleeve decreases.

Sleeve Decrease
Rows 1 to 5: Knit row (following color chart), slipping marker. Work MC after chart is completed.
Row 6: K2tog after marker and again before marker at end of row.
Repeat rows 1 to 6 until sleeve inseam measures; 14 (14, 15, 15, 16)". On last row you may need to decrease sts to have a multiple of 6 sts. Change to smaller size 6 or dp needles and knit cuff ribbing

Cuff Ribbing
K3, p3 lining up the knit and purl sts; repeat continuously for 2". Bind off loosely. Slip stitches on needles over to other sleeve section between markers 3 and 4. Attach yarn and repeat for other sleeve.

Body
All sts will be joined to knit body circular. Continue following color chart as was done for the sleeves. When joining at sleeve inseam, pick up 2 to 3 sts from underarm on each side to close gap. On next round, k2tog; 2 or 3 times to decrease these extra sts. Knit body circular for 10 (11, 11, 12, 13)" or desired length measuring from underarm. Make sure you have a multiple of 6 stitches. Change to smaller needles.

Cuff
Work 2" of k3, p3 ribbing to match neck and cuffs. Bind off loosely.

Finishing
Weave in loose ends. If there is a hole in underarm, sew closed with yarn. Block.

Color Chart Key

	MC-tan
g	Gold
b	Blue
P	Plum
G	Green
B	Black

Color Chart

Work each row from right to left.

B			1
B	B		2
	B	B	3
b	b	b	4
b	b	b	5
	g	b	6
	b	g	7
g	g	g	8
g	g	B	9
B	g	B	10
B	B	g	11
P	B	B	12
P	P	P	13
	g	P	14
	P	g	15
	g		16
			17
			18
		G	19
	g	g	20
		b	21
b	b	b	22
	b	G	23
	G	G	24
		G	25
g	g	g	26
G	G	G	27
P	P	P	28
B	P		29
b	B		30
B	b		31
b	g	b	32
g			33
		g	34

Finished measurements of sweater

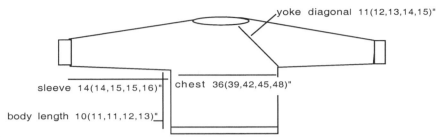

yoke diagonal 11(12,13,14,15)"

sleeve 14(14,15,15,16)"

chest 36(39,42,45,48)"

body length 10(11,11,12,13)"

Measurements do not include ribbing.

10½

Knit'n Hood
Make It and Keep It

Keep warm and dry on a cool day with this hooded cardigan. This sweater is knit from the top down and the hood is knit after the sweater is completed. Sweater pictured was knit holding two strands of dk weight yarn together for the equivalent of a worsted weight yarn. Select fun yarn and knit this simple cardigan with or without a hood.

Sizes

Sweater is written for sizes; **small, medium, large, x--large and xx--large.** Directions are written for size small with larger sizes in parenthesis.

Sweater pictured knit with Wendy Romany dk (double strand)

Finished Chest Measurements With Button Band Overlapped.

Chest circumference 40 (43, 46, 49, 52)"

Materials

Yarn Worsted weight total yardage 1200 (1300, 1450, 1600, 1800) yds.
Circular Needles One pair each size 6 and 10 16" length. Size 10 24" length.
Double Point Needles Size 6 and 10 can also be used for the sleeves.
Markers
Tapestry Needle
Buttons

Gauge

4 to 5 sts and 6 to 7 rows = 1" working Stockinette st knit with worsted yarn and s
Gauge may vary with different yarn.

Neck Ribbing

With size 6 circular needles cast on 100 (104, 108, 112, 116) sts, turn.
k2, p2, ribbing across row, turn. Repeat k2, p2 ribbing lining up the knit sts and purl sts for 2".
On last row (RS), increase 2 sts on last row. (Place increases in the ribbing about 1/3 and 2/3
around.)

Optional Short Row Explanation and Directions to be worked starting on row 4.

4 optional short rows may be added to the back and part of the sleeve sections of the sweater for
a more comfortable fit. Short rows are knit after neck ribbing is finished and you have changed to
larger needles. WS, Slip beg marker (1st marker) and purl to the 4th marker. P2 sts past 4th
marker, yarn back (yb), sl 1, yarn forward (yf), turn work to (RS), sl 1 st, knit to beg marker,
knit 2 sts past beg marker, yf, sl 1, yb, turn work, (WS), sl 1st, purl to where last turn was made
(2 sts past the 4th marker) purl 2 sts past last short row turn, yb, sl 1 st, yf, turn work, (RS), sl
1 st, knit to end of row. Work row 5 of yoke next.

M1 Make 1 stitch: On knit side, with left needles, pick up the horizontal strand between last st
and next st to be knit, pick it up from front to back and knit into the back of this strand with the
right needle. Strand is twisted to avoid a hole. See pattern notes for detailed pictures.

Yoke

(RS) Change to larger size 10 circular needles and place the markers as follows:
k17 (18, 18, 19, 20), place marker, k18 (19, 20, 20, 21), place marker,
k 30 (30, 32, 34, 34), place marker, k18 (19, 20, 20, 21), place marker,
k17 (18, 18, 19, 20), turn.
Row 1 and all odd rows: Purl.
Row 2: Knit row and at same time M1   2 sts before and after each marker.
Row 4: *If short rows are going to be worked, begin them on this row. After short rows are
worked continue with instructions.* WS, Knit row and at same time work a M1   6 sts before and
after each marker, turn.
Row 6: M1   2 sts before and after markers.
Row 10 and every even row: Continue to work M1 before and after markers , changing the
placement of the M1 on each row. By altering their placement, there will be no raglan line. You
can place them farther away from the markers as more sts are added. When yoke measures: 11
(12, 13, 14, 15)", end (WS) the wrong side is the last row worked.

Sleeve

Knit across to the first sleeve marker between beg marker and 2nd marker, begin using the size 10 16" circular needles, or size 10 dp needles. Knit sleeve sts on new needles, join to knit circular, place a marker where the two edges of the sleeve join. Continue knitting sleeve circular with the following inseam decreases.

Rows 1 to 5: Knit.

Row 6: K2tog before and after marker.

Continue to knit 5 rows and decrease 2 sts on 6th row until sleeve is the desired length, or 15 (15, 16, 16, 17)". Change to smaller size 6 16" circular needles or dp needles for cuff. Make sure you have a multiple of 4 sts for cuff.

Cuff

Work k2, p2, ribbing for 2" lining up the k sts and p sts. Bind off loosely.

Slip sts over to other sleeve section between markers 3 and 4. Attach yarn and repeat for other sleeve.

Body

All remaining sts will be connected for body of sweater. Pick up 2 to 3 sts under each sleeve to close gap. (See front instructions) Knit body in Stockinette stitch until it measures 12 (12, 13, 13, 14)" or desired length without the ribbing. Make sure you have a multiple of 4 sts.

Cuff

Change to smaller size 6 circular needles and work a k2, p2, ribbing lining up the knit sts and purl sts for 2". Bind off loosely.

Hood

Hood is added after sweater is finished and before button bands are knit. Attach yarn on first stitch of cast on row on RS and with size 6 needles, pick up 1 st per cast on stitch around neck; 100 (104, 108, 112, 116) sts. Turn.

Row 1: Purl row, turn

Row 2: Knit row, turn.

Row 3: K4, purl to last 4 sts, k4, turn.

Row 4: P4, knit to last 4 sts, p4, turn.

Change to larger size 10 needles and continue repeating rows 1 to 4 until hood measures 13" or measurement of head from neck to top of head. Place half of the hood sts on another dp or circular needle so the center of the hood can be folded and the two rows of stitches can be knit together. Fold hood in half with right sides together. Knit both sides together at the same time by knitting through both sts from both needles at once. This will bind off both edges of hood and sew them together.

Front Band

With smaller size 6 needles, pick up 1 st per row along front right side edge picking up sts from the bottom edge to the cast on row and work a k2, p2, ribbing for 1 to 2" working button holes every 3" on right band (see buttonholes following). Work matching button band on other front.

Buttonholes

Work button band to where you want a buttonhole, bind off 2 sts where you want a buttonhole. On next row back, cast on 2 sts where the 2 previous sts were bound off. Bind off 3 sts for a larger hole, then cast on 3 sts.

Finishing

Weave in yarn ends, sew on buttons and if needed work a small blanket stitch around each buttonhole for reinforcement. A crocheted edge can also be worked around the outside edges of finished sweater. Block sweater with water mist and press with hands.

Finished sweater measurements

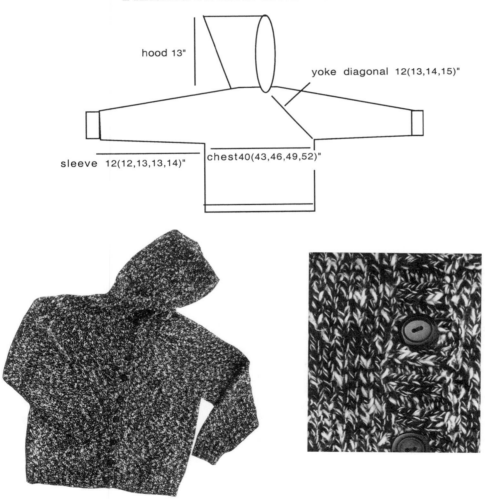

hood 13"

yoke diagonal 12(13,14,15)"

sleeve 12(12,13,13,14)"

chest 40(43,46,49,52)"

Button Up
Up Up and Away

A combination of increases and decreases makes a lacy ribbing to edge this pullover sweater. The front placket opening in this sweater makes it easy and comfortable to wear. Knit with nubby two toned yarn, this solid seamless sweater is very comfortable, loose fitting and versatile.

Sizes

Sweater is written for sizes; **small, medium, large, x-large, and xx-large.** Directions are written for smallest size with larger sizes in parenthesis.

Sweater pictured was knit with Wendy Romany dk yarn.

Finished Chest Measurements

Chest circumference 38 (41, 44, 47, 50)"

Materials

Yarn dk weight nubby total yardage needed 1050 (1150, 1250, 1450, 1700) yds.
Circular Needles One pair each size 4 and 8   16" length, one pair size 8 24" length.
3 Buttons
Markers

Gauge

5 to 6 sts = 1" 7 to 8 rows = 1" Stockinette st knit with Romany dk weight yarn and size 8 needles. Gauge may vary depending on yarn and texture used.

24

Neck Ribbing

With size 4 needles and MC cast on 102 (106, 110, 114, 118) sts. Turn.

Row 1: K1, *p2, k2*; rep between *'s, turn, end k1. Note: A k2,p2, ribbing can be worked for row 2 also, in place of the one written for this sweater.

Row 2 and every row of ribbing: K1, *k2tog tbl, (through back loop) yb (this is the same as a yo for the purl st), p2,* rep between *'s to end, k1. Work buttonhole 1" from cast on edge (see ribbing and placket buttonholes following).

Ribbing and Placket Buttonholes

Work button hole by knitting 3 sts on edge, then binding off the next 2 sts. On next row, cast on 2 sts where 2 previous sts were bound off. Continue buttonholes every 1 1/2" or as often as desired down the front placket band after ribbing is worked. When ribbing measures 2 (2, 2, 3, 3)" change to larger size 8 24" needles.

Preparatory Row K17 (18, 19, 19, 20), place marker, k19 (20, 20, 22, 22), place marker, k30 (30, 32, 32, 34), place marker, k19 (20, 20, 22, 22), place marker, k17 (18, 19, 19, 20), turn. **Note** Work the first 5 sts on both edges of placket in garter stitch, knit first and last 5 sts on every row both knit and purl sides.

Optional Short Row Explanation and Directions to be worked starting on row 4. (If you don't want to work short rows, begin with yoke directions) 4 optional short rows may be added to the back and part of the sleeve sections of the sweater for a more comfortable fit. Short rows are knit after neck ribbing is finished and you have changed to larger needles. WS, Slip beg marker (1st marker) and purl to the 4th marker. P2 sts past 4th marker, yarn back (yb), sl 1, yarn forward (yf), turn work to (RS), sl 1 st, knit to beg marker, knit 2 sts past beg marker, yf, sl 1, yb, turn work, (WS), sl 1st, purl to where last turn was made (2 sts past the 4th marker) purl 2 sts past last short row turn, yb, sl 1 st, yf, turn work, (RS), sl 1 st, knit to end of row.

M1 Make 1 stitch: On knit side, with left needles, pick up the horizontal strand between last st and next st to be knit, pick it up from front to back and knit into the back of this strand with the right needle. Strand is twisted to avoid a hole. See pattern notes for detailed pictures. **Note** To keep track of increase rows, wrap beg marker twice to indicate increase row, once on non increase rows.

Yoke

Row 1:RS, Knit row and M1 2 sts before and after markers.

Row 2 and all even rows: K first and last 5 sts, purl row. Follow short row directions on row 4 if you are working them.

Row 3: Rep row 1 and at same time M1 6 sts before and after markers.

Row 5: Knit row and at same time M1 3 sts before and after markers.

Row 7: Knit row and at same time M1 1 st before and after marker.

Continue increasing sts on all odd rows in yoke, placing M1 different numbers of sts from markers so increases don't line up. When placket opening is 3 to 4" or desired length, join placket front.

Placket Front

(RS) Place 5 sts from buttonhole side band on dp needle, overlap with 5 sts from other side so buttonhole edge is on top. Knit both sets of 5 sts together to join and overlap. Continue to knit the rest of yoke circular and continue with increase pattern every odd row until yoke measures: 11 (12, 13, 14, 15)" not including the ribbing.

Sleeve

Knit over to sleeve section which is between the beg marker and the 2nd marker and leave all other sts on longer needle. Knit sleeve section on 16" size 8 needle or dp needles. Knit over sleeve section, join to knit circular and place marker where sleeve is joined.

Rows 1 to 5: Knit row.

Row 6: K2 sts together before and after marker and knit remaining row.

Repeat rows 1 to 6 until sleeve inseam measures 14 (14, 15, 15, 16)" or desired sleeve length without cuff.

Cuff

Change to smaller size 4 16" circular or dp needles. Make sure you have remaining cuff sts divisible by 4.

Row 1: K2, p2; rep around.

Row 2: K2tog tbl, yb (yo for purl), p2; rep around. You can work a k2, p2, ribbing instead.

Repeat rows 1 and 2 for 2". Bind off loosely. Slip sts over to other sleeve section between the 3rd and 4th markers, tie on yarn and repeat sleeve directions for second sleeve.

Body

Join front and back sections to knit circular. To close gap under arm inseam, pick up 2 to 3 sts from sleeve inseam sts. On next round, k2tog 2 or 3 times to decrease these added sts. When body measures 10 (10, 11, 11, 12)" or desired length decrease 10 sts on last row, change to smaller size 4 needles.

Ribbing

Work same ribbing as for cuff and neck ribbing over a multiple of 4 sts. When ribbing measures 3", Bind off loosely.

Finishing

Weave in loose ends with tapestry needle and block. Sew on buttons work a blanket stitch around buttonholes for reinforcement. A blanket stitch may also be worked around placket edge.

Finished sweater measurements

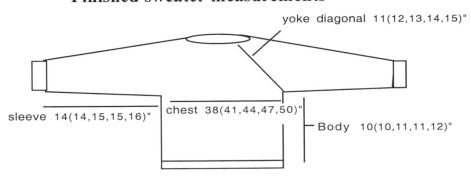

yoke diagonal 11(12,13,14,15)"

sleeve 14(14,15,15,16)"   chest 38(41,44,47,50)"

Body 10(10,11,11,12)"

27

Just Peachy
Creamy and Sweet

Combine a peachy textured yarn with a blend of lavender, off white and solid peach for a subtle yoke and comfortable sweater. Three quarter length sleeves add a charm to this sweater. Increases are hidden in the colors of the yoke for a delicate impression.

Sizes
Sweater is written for sizes; **small, medium, large, x--large, xx--large.** Instructions are for size small with larger sizes in parenthesis.

Sweater pictured was knit with a cotton boucle' yarn

Finished Chest Measurements
Chest circumference 36 (39, 42, 45, 48)"

Materials
Yarn Worsted weight nubby yarn total yardage needed of Main color : 1000 (1100, 1200, 1400, 1700) yds.
1 skein of 3 contrasting colors
Circular Needles One pair each size 4 and 8 16 length, size 8 24" length.
Double Point Size 4 and 8 can be used instead of the 16" circular needles.
Markers

Gauge

4 sts and 5 to 6 rows = 1" working Stockinette stitch with size 8 needles and boucle' yarn. Gauge may vary with different yarns.

Note Since yarn may be textured and sometimes uneven, gauge will vary depending on where sample is measured. Size is determined by the length of the yoke, if a larger sweater is desired, knit yoke longer 1" = 1 more size or 3" on chest measurement.

Neck Ribbing

Cast on 90 (96, 100, 106, 110) sts on size 4 needles, join with beginning to knit circular, be careful not to twist stitches.

Rows 1 and all odd rows: K1, p1; rep around.
Row 2 and all even rows: K1, p1; rep around.
Repeat rows 1 and 2 for 2".
Change to larger size 8 24" needles.

Preparatory Row: K17 (18, 19, 21, 22), place marker (sleeve), k28 (30, 31, 32, 33), place marker (back), k17 (18, 19, 21, 22) place marker (sleeve), k28 (30, 31, 32, 33), place marker (front), beginning marker is a different color of yarn tied in slip knot large enough to wrap around needle once or twice. Keep track of increase rows by wrapping yarn twice, which indicates an increase row. Once around means no increase.

Optional short rows explanation to be started on row 4. (If you don't want to work short rows, begin with yoke directions below.) Four optional short rows are explained here and may be knit after neck ribbing is finished and you have changed to larger needles. (RS) Slip beg marker (1st marker) and knit to the 4th marker. K2 sts past 4th marker, yf, sl 1, yb, turn work to(WS), sl 1 st, purl to beg marker, purl 2 sts past beg marker, yb, sl 1, yf, turn work, (RS), sl 1st, knit to where last turn was made (2 sts past the 4th marker) knit 2 sts past last short row turn, yf, sl 1 st, yb, turn work, (WS) sl 1 st, purl to beg marker, purl 4 sts past beg marker. yb, sl 1, yf, turn work, (RS) sl 1 st, knit to beg marker.   You have just added 4 rows to the back and part of the sleeve sections of the sweater for a more comfortable fit.

M1 Make 1 stitch: On knit side, with left needles, pick up the horizontal strand between last st and next st to be knit, pick it up from front to back and knit into the back of this strand with the right needle. Strand is twisted to avoid a hole. See pattern notes for detailed pictures. **Note** The M1 stitch is scattered so they do not line up for the seamless effect.

Begin color chart row 1 and start row 1 of pattern.

Row 1: M1 4 sts before and after markers to beg marker.
Row 2 and all even rows: Knit

29

Row 3: Rep row 2 except M1 6 sts before and after markers.

Row 5: M1 8 sts before and after markers.

Row 7: M1 10 sts before and after markers.

Rep this M1 pattern every other row changing number of sts knit before and after markers keeping the number of sts the same distance from each marker for that row. As the yoke gets longer, you can M1 st farther from markers until front yoke measures: 11 (12, 13, 14, 15)" not including ribbing. End at beg marker.

Note With shorter size 8 16" needles, begin knitting over sleeve sts, which should be from the beginning marker to the 2nd marker, keeping all other sts on longer needles to be knit later. With shorter needles join sleeve sts to knit sleeves circular. Place marker between beginning and end of sleeves sts for inseam .

Sleeves

Rows 1 to 5: Knit

Row 6: K2tog before and after marker and knit rest of row.

Repeat this pattern rows 1 to 6 until sleeve inseam measures 10 (10, 11, 11, 12)" or desired length ending with an even number of sts.   Change to smaller size 4 16" or dp needles.

Cuff

Row 1: K, p1; rep around.

Continue repeating row 1 lining up knit and purl sts until cuff measures 2". Bind off loosely.

Slip stitches over to other sleeve section which is between the 3rd and 4th markers. Follow same directions for second sleeve.

Body

All sts will be joined to knit body circular. When joining at sleeve inseam, pick up 2 to 3 sts from underarm on each side to close gap. On next row, k2tog 2 to 3 times to decrease added sts.

Knit body 12 (12, 13, 13, 14)" or desired length. Change to smaller size 4 needles. Make sure you have an even number of sts remaining.

Cuff

Row 1: K1, p1; rep around. Rep row 1 lining up k sts and p sts for 2" . Bind off loosely.

Finishing

Weave in loose ends with tapestry needle and block.

Color Chart Key

Begin on right side of each row. Each size stops on chart when yoke length is reached, finish 1 or 2 rows of that color.

n	Natural
p	peach
a	Apricot
l	Lavender

Measurements for finished sweater

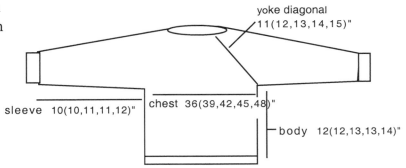

yoke diagonal
11(12,13,14,15)"

sleeve 10(10,11,11,12)"

chest 36(39,42,45,48)"

body 12(12,13,13,14)"

Color Chart for "Just Peachy"

Begin with row 1 and start each row from the right and work to the left side.

				#					#					#					#
p	p	p	p	1	l	a	a	a	24	a	a	a	a	47	n	n	a	n	70
p	p	p	p	2	l	l	a	l	25	a	a	a	n	48	n	n	a	n	71
p	p	p	p	3	l	l	l	l	26	a	n	n	n	49	n	n	n	n	72
p	p	p	p	4	l	l	l	l	27	n	n	n	n	50	n	n	n	n	73
n	p	p	p	5	l	l	l	l	28	n	n	n	n	51	n	n	n	n	74
n	n	p	n	6	n	l	l	l	29	n	n	n	n	52	n	n	n	n	75
n	n	n	n	7	n	n	l	n	30	n	n	n	n	53	l	p	l	p	76
n	n	n	n	8	n	n	n	n	31	l	n	n	n	54	l	p	l	p	77
n	n	n	n	9	n	n	n	n	32	l	l	n	l	55	p	p	p	p	78
n	n	n	n	10	n	n	n	n	33	l	l	l	l	56	p	p	p	p	79
n	n	n	n	11	n	n	n	n	34	l	l	l	l	57	p	p	p	p	80
n	n	n	n	12	n	n	n	n	35	l	l	l	l	58	a	p	p	p	81
l	n	n	n	13	n	n	n	n	36	l	l	l	l	59	a	a	p	a	82
l	l	n	l	14	n	n	n	n	37	l	l	l	l	60	a	a	a	a	83
l	l	l	l	15	l	n	l	n	38	l	l	l	l	61	a	a	a	a	84
l	l	l	l	16	l	n	l	n	39	a	l	l	l	62	n	a	a	a	85
l	l	l	l	17	n	n	n	n	40	a	a	l	a	63	n	n	a	n	86
l	l	l	l	18	n	n	n	n	41	a	a	l	a	64	n	n	n	n	87
l	l	l	l	19	p	n	n	n	42	a	a	a	a	65	n	n	n	n	88
a	l	l	l	20	p	p	n	p	43	a	a	a	a	66	l	n	n	n	89
a	a	l	a	21	p	p	p	p	44	a	a	a	a	67	l	l	n	l	90
a	a	a	a	22	p	p	p	p	45	a	a	a	a	68	l	l	l	l	91
a	a	a	a	23	p	p	p	a	46	a	a	a	a	69	a	l	l	l	92

Ripple Knits'Kin

It Might Turn Into gold

This spring sweater is knit from the top down with waves flowing from the neck down. Increases and decreases combine to make waves. Yoke increases are hidden into the wave for a smooth appearance. A picot edge is the final touch for a light spring feeling.

Sizes

Sweater is written for sizes; **small, medium, large, x-large and xx-large.** Sweater instructions are written for size small with larger sizes in parenthesis.

Sweater pictured was knit with Mexican Wave dk yarn.

Finished Chest Measurements

Chest circumference 36 (39, 42, 45, 48)"

Materials

Yarn dk or sport weight total yardage main color: 900 (1100, 1200, 1400, 1600) yds.
Contrasting stripes: 1 skein
Circular Needles One pair each size 6 and 8 16" length and size 6 and 8 24" lengths. DP needles can also be used for shorter 16" needles.
Tapestry Needle
Markers

Gauge

5 to 6 sts and 7 to 8 rows = 1" Stockinette st, knit with size 8 needles and Mexican Wave dk weight yarn. Gauge may vary with different yarns.

Top Neck Edge

(Twisted after several rows of Stockinette st are worked.)

With size 6 circular needles cast on 96 (96, 96, 120, 120) sts, turn.

Row 1: (RS) Knit row, turn.

Row 2: (WS) Purl row, turn.

Rep rows 1 and 2; 3 more times. (8 rows total.)

Twist Row: (RS) *K4, twist work by holding these 4 stitches on right hand needle and wrap needle and sts behind, back, down and around up front to twist the row.* Think of this motion like the right pedal of a bicycle, it will go around and back, down and forward, up to the top, k4*. Rep between *'s to the end of the row. The throw yarn will get tangled as you do this, be patient and keep it straight as you do the "twist". Join to knit circular, place beginning marker, where sts are joined. Make sure row is not twisted, although, there are many twists worked.

Ribbing Rows 1 to 8: K4, p4; rep around slipping marker as you knit.

Optional short rows explanation to be started on row 4. (If you don't want to work short rows, begin with yoke directions below.) Four optional short rows are explained here and may be knit after neck ribbing is finished and you have changed to larger needles. (RS) Slip beg marker (1st marker) and knit to the 4th marker. K2 sts past 4th marker, yf, sl 1, yb, turn work to(WS), sl 1 st, purl to beg marker, purl 2 sts past beg marker, yb, sl 1, yf, turn work, (RS), sl 1st, knit to where last turn was made (2 sts past the 4th marker) knit 2 sts past last short row turn, yf, sl 1 st, yb, turn work, (WS) sl 1 st, purl to beg marker, purl 4 sts past beg marker. yb, sl 1, yf, turn work, (RS) sl 1 st, knit to beg marker. You have just added 4 rows to the back and part of the sleeve sections of the sweater for a more comfortable fit.

Yoke

Row 1: (Marker may need to be moved a stitch or two as pattern is knit to keep it at the beginning of the wave.) With larger size 8 16" needles, k1, replace beginning marker, *yo, k1, k3tog, k1, yo, k1*; rep between *'s 16 (16, 16, 20, 20) times, end at beg marker.

Rows 2 and 3: Knit.

Row 4: (Increase row, make sure k3tog line up with previous k3 worked from row 1.) Slip beginning marker, *yo, k1inc, k3tog, k1inc, yo, k1*. Rep between *'s, 32 (32, 32, 40, 40) sts increased.

Rows 5 & 6: Knit

Row 7 & 10: Slip marker, *yo, k2, k3tog, k2, yo, k1*; rep around.

Rows 8 & 9: knit.

Row 11 & 12: Knit

Row 13: (Increase row) Slip marker, *yo, k7, yo, k1*; rep around.

Rows 14 & 15: Knit

Rows 16 & 19: Slip marker, *yo, k3, k3tog, k3, yo, k1*; rep around.

Rows 17 & 18: Knit

Rows 20 & 21: Knit

Row 22: (Increase row) Slip marker, *yo, k9, yo, k1*; rep around.

Rows 23 & 24: Knit

Rows 25 & 28: Slip marker, *yo, k4, k3tog, k4, yo, k1*; rep around.

Rows26 & 27: Knit

Rows 29 & 30: Knit

Row 31: (Increase row) Slip marker, *yo, k11, yo, k1*; rep around.

Rows 32 & 33: Knit

Rows 34 & 37: Slip marker, *yo, k5, k3tog, k5, yo, k1*; rep around.

Rows35 & 36: Knit

Rows 38 & 39: Knit

Row 40: Slip marker, *yo, k13, yo, k1*; rep around.

Rows 41 & 42: Knit

Rows 43 & 46: Slip marker, *yo, k6, k3tog, k6, yo, k1*; rep around.

Rows 44 & 45: Knit

Rows 47 & 48: Knit

Row 49: Slip marker, *yo, k15, yo, k1*; rep around.

Rows 50 & 51: Knit

Rows 52 & 55: Slip marker, *yo, k7, k3tog, k7, yo, k1*; rep around.

Rows 53 & 54: Knit

Rows 56 & 57: Knit

Row 58: Slip marker, *yo, k17, yo, k1*; rep around.

Rows 59 & 60: Knit

Rows 61 & 64: Slip marker, *yo, k8, k3tog, k8, yo, k1*; rep around.

Rows 62 & 63: Knit

Rows 65 & 66: Knit

Row 67: slip marker, *yo, k19, yo, k1*; rep around.

Rows 68 & 69: Knit

Rows 70 and 73: Slip marker, *yo, k9, k3tog, k8, yo, k1*; rep around.

Rows 71 & 72: Knit

Rows 74 & 75: Knit.

You may need to continue in this pattern increasing sts every 9th row until yoke measures 11 (12, 13, 14, 15)"

Note One wave is the area from after the k1 to before the next k1. There are 16 (16, 16, 20, 20) waves total.

Sleeves

Sleeve will be worked over 4 (4, 4, 5, 5) waves. Change to smaller size 8 16" circular needles, or dp needles. Begin sleeve section from beginning marker and work 4 (4, 4, 5, 5) waves after beg marker. Join sleeve section to knit circular. Place marker where sts join. Continue with established pattern of yo's and k3tog, separated with 2 knit rows without making any more increases as was done in the yoke. When sleeve inseam measures 3" begin sleeve decrease.

Sleeve Decrease

On every yo and k3tog row, do not work yo at sleeve inseam once on either side of the marker, this will decrease the sleeve by 2 sts each time this row is worked. Knit 4 (4, 5, 5, 6)" more, or desired length. Change to smaller size 6 16" circular needles, or dp size 6 needles to work cuff circular.

Cuff

You should have a number of sts in multiples of 8. Sts may need to be decreased or added.
Rows 1 to 6: K4, p4; rep around.
Row 5: Scallop edge; Bind off 2 sts, place remaining st on left needle, cast on 2 sts on stitch just placed on right needle, dec next 4 sts including 2 sts just added. Rep around.
For the second sleeve, slip sts past 4 (4, 4, 5, 5) waves, attach yarn and repeat instructions for other sleeve.

Body

Remaining sts are body. Join at sides to knit circular. Continue working the established pattern of k3tog's and yo's with 2 knit rows in between for 10 (11, 11, 12, 13)", or desired length. Make sure there is a multiple of 8 sts for body cuff. Change to smaller size 6 needles, and work cuff in k4, p4 for 1 inch. Bind off in scallop edge as was done on row 5 of sleeve cuff.

Finishing

With tapestry needle, close gap at neck edge, under arm inseam and cuff edging. When blocking sweater, shape the edges to follow the wave pattern.

Finished sweater measurements

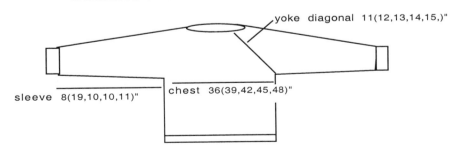

yoke diagonal 11(12,13,14,15,)"

sleeve 8(19,10,10,11)"

chest 36(39,42,45,48)"

Knitting the Waves

You Won't Get Wet

Flowing waves hide the yoke increases as they subtly widen over the shoulders. A mixture of knit three stitches together and decreases blend for the waves. Choose your favorite colors and with worsted weight yarn, this is a winter warmer sweater.

Sizes

Sweater is written for sizes; **small, medium, large, x-large, xx-large,**. Instructions are written for size small with larger sizes in parenthesis.

Sweater pictured knit with Patons Classic Wool worsted weight.

Finished Chest Measurements

Chest circumference 36 (39, 42, 45, 48)"

Materials

Yarn Worsted weight total yardage needed of Main color; 1050 (1150, 1250, 1450, 1700) yds, 50 grams each of Burgundy, Green, Gold, Blue, or colors of your choice.

Circular Needles One pair each size 4 and 8 16" length, size 8 24" length. Size 4 and 8 double point needles can be substituted for the 16" needles for the neck and cuffs.

Tapestry Needle

Markers

Gauge

4 to 5 sts and 6 to 7 rows = 1 inch knit in Stockinette st knit with size 8 needles and Patons Classic wool. Gauge will vary with different yarn.

Top Neck Edge

With size 4 16" circular needles and MC cast on 100 (100, 100, 120,120,120) sts, join to knit circular making sure stitches are not twisted. Place marker when joining, this will be your beg marker. Always slip beg marker and start each row from the that marker.

Row 1: (RS) K3, p2; rep across row, turn.

Row 2: K1, sl 1, k1, p2; rep across row. Make sure you line up the p2 sts. Rep rows 1 and 2 until ribbing measures 2". Note: A k3, p2, ribbing can be worked for entire ribbing. Change to larger size 8 16" circular needles.

Body

Check off each row as it is knit to keep track of where you are. Post--it's also work well to keep track of where you are. Follow color chart as you follow pattern. Rows of color chart and pattern line up, row 1 to row 1.

____ **Row 1:** *K1inc, k3tog, k1inc, * Multiples of 5 sts. Rep around, end at beginning marker. There will be 20 (20, 20, 24, 24, 24) sections total.

____**Rows 2 & all even rows:** Knit.

____**Row 3:** (Inc row) Make sure k3 (not together) line up with previous k3tog worked. Slip marker, *k1 inc, k3, k1 inc, * Rep around. 40 sts increased.

____**Rows 5,7,9,11:** *K1 inc, k1, k3tog, k1, k1 inc, * rep around.

____**Row 13:** *K1inc, k5, k1inc,* rep around. 40 sts increased.

____**Rows 15,17,19, 21:** *K1inc, k2, k3tog, k2, k1inc,* rep around.

____**Row 23:** *K1inc, k7, k1inc,* rep around. 40 sts increased.

____**Rows 25,27,29,31:** *k1inc, k3, k3tog, k3, k1inc,* rep around.

____**Row 33:** *K1inc, k9, k1inc,* rep around. 40 sts increased.

____**Rows 35,37,39,41:** *K1inc, k4, k3tog, k4, k1inc,* rep around.

____**Row 43:** *K1inc, k11, k1inc,* rep around.

____**Rows 45,47,49,51:** *K1inc, k5, k3tog, k5, k1inc,* rep around.

____**Row 53:** *K1inc, k13, k1inc,* rep around. (End size small)

____**Rows 55,57,59,61:** *K1inc, k6, k3tog, k6, k1inc,* rep around.

____**Row 63:** *K1inc, k15, k1inc,* rep around. (End size med)

____**Rows 65,67 69,71:** *K1inc, k7, k3tog, k7, k1inc,* rep around.

____**Row 73:** *K1inc, k17, k1inc,* rep around. (End size large)

____**Rows 75,77,79,81:** *K1inc, k8, k3tog, k8, k1inc,* rep around.

____**Row 83:** *K1inc, k19, k1inc,* rep around.(End size x--large)

____**Rows 85,87,89,91:** *K1inc, k9, k3tog, k9, k1inc,* rep around.

___**Row 93:** *K1inc, k21, k1inc,* rep around.(End size xx--large)
___**Rows 95,97,99,101:** *K1inc, k10, k3tog, k10, k1inc,* rep around.
___**Row 103:** *K1inc, k23, k1inc,* rep around. (End xxx--large)

Note One wave is the area from before a k1inc to after a k1inc.

Sleeves
With shorter 16" size 8 needles, work sleeves over 4 (4, 4, 5, 5, 5) wave sections, place marker where the beginning and end of sleeve are joined and this will become the sleeve inseam. Continue in established pattern of k1 inc's and k3tog's, except at the arm inseam. Only work 1 k1 inc at each side of marker every other row so sleeve doesnt widen.

Sleeve Inseam Decrease
K2tog before and after marker every 6th row of sleeve inseam. Work 3 rows of green and 2 rows of red before working cuff. When sleeve length measures 14 (14, 15, 15, 16, 16)", change to smaller size 4 needles or dp size 4 needles to work cuff circular. Make sure you have a multiple of 5 stitches remaining.

Cuff
Row 1: K3, p2; rep around.
Row 2: K1, sl 1, k1, p2; rep around.
Rep rows 1 & 2 until cuff measures 3" bind off loosely.
Slip sts past 6 (6, 6, 7, 7, 7) wave sections. Slip the same number of sts as the first sleeve on needle for other sleeve. Before you knit it, count the number of sts on front and back to make sure they are close to the same in number. Attach yarn after sts are slipped. Repeat for other sleeve.

Body
Remaining sts are body. Join front and back, picking up 2 to 3 sts under arm inseam on first round. On second round, k2tog, 2 or 3 times to decrease these sts, so wave pattern will continue. Continue established pattern of k3tog's and yo's until body length measures 10 (11, 11, 12, 12, 13)" or desired length. Make sure you have a multiple of 5 sts remaining. Change to smaller size 4 needles and decrease 10 sts evenly around first row.

Body Ribbing
Row 1: K3, p2; rep around lining up knit and purl sts until cuff measures 2". Bind off loosely.

Finishing
With tapestry needle, weave in ends. Spray with water mist and press with hands.

Color Chart Key

t	tan
g	green
y	yellow
r	red
b	blue

Finished sweater measurements

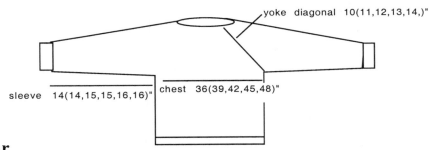

yoke diagonal 10(11,12,13,14,)"

sleeve 14(14,15,15,16,16)"   chest 36(39,42,45,48)"

Color Chart for Knittin' the Waves

Start color chart from row 1 and reading each row from right to left, work chart until yoke is desired length .

t	t	1	r	r	16	t	t	31	t	t	46	t	t	61	g	g	76	y	y	91
t	t	2	t	t	17	t	t	32	t	t	47	t	t	62	g	g	77	y	y	92
t	t	3	t	t	18	g	g	33	t	t	48	r	r	63	g	g	78	y	y	93
g	g	4	t	t	19	g	g	34	b	b	49	r	r	64	y	y	79	y	y	94
g	g	5	t	t	20	g	g	35	b	b	50	y	y	65	y	y	80	g	g	95
g	g	6	t	t	21	g	g	36	b	b	51	y	y	66	b	b	81	g	g	96
g	g	7	t	t	22	r	r	37	b	b	52	b	b	67	b	b	82	t	t	97
t	t	8	t	t	23	r	r	38	t	t	53	b	b	68	r	r	83	t	t	98
t	t	9	b	b	24	y	y	39	t	t	54	b	b	69	r	r	88	t	t	99
t	t	10	b	b	25	y	y	40	g	g	55	b	b	70	t	t	85	t	t	100
y	y	11	t	t	26	r	r	41	g	g	56	t	t	71	t	t	86	b	b	101
y	y	12	t	t	27	r	r	42	g	g	57	t	t	72	t	t	87	b	b	102
y	y	13	b	b	28	y	y	43	r	r	58	t	t	73	t	t	88	b	b	103
y	y	14	b	b	29	y	y	44	r	r	59	t	t	74	r	r	89	t	t	104
r	r	15	t	t	30	y	y	45	t	t	60	t	t	75	r	r	90	t	t	105

Flowered Cables

Cardigan with Climbing Vines

Cables flowing from the neck down, with yoke increases hidden before and after the cables for a smooth appearance. Flowers are embroidered on after sweater is completed. A blanket stitch embroidered edge frames this cardigan for the final touch.

Sizes

Instructions are written for sizes; **small**, **medium**, **large**, **x-large and xx-large.** Directions are for size small with larger sizes in parenthesis.

Sweater pictured knit with Patons Shetland Ragg yarn.

Finished Chest Measurements

Measured with buttonhole band overlapped as if buttoned.
Chest circumference 40 (43, 46, 49, 52)"

Materials

Yarn Worsted weight total yardage needed; 1000 (1100, 1200, 1400, 1600) yds.
Remnants of variegated and plain green yarn for embroidery
Circular Needles One pair each size 4 and 8 16"length. Size 8 24" length. Size 4 and 8 dp needles can also be used for sleeves and cuff.
Tapestry Needle
8 Buttons or number of button holes.

Gauge
4 to 5 sts and 7 rows = 1" Stockinette st knit with size 8 needles and Shetland Ragg yarn. Gauge may vary with different yarn.

Top Neck Edge
With size 4 circular needles cast on: 87 (87, 100, 100, 100) sts, turn.

Row 1: (RS) P3 (3, 4, 4, 4), k4; rep around end p3 (3, 4, 4, 4), turn.

Rows 2 & 4: (WS) K3 (3, 4, 4, 4), k4; rep around, ending k3 (3, 4, 4, 4).

Row 3: P3 (3, 4, 4, 4), k4; rep around, ending p3 (3, 4, 4, 4), turn.

Row 5: * P3 (3, 4, 4, 4), 4 stitch left cable, (slip 2 sts to cable needle, hold to back of work, k next 2 sts, k 2 sts from cable needle.)* rep bet *'s 5 more times. * p3, 4 stitch left cable, (slip 2 sts to cable needle hold to front of work, knit next 2 sts, knit 2 sts from cable needle) * rep between last *'s 5 more times, end p3, turn.

Rep rows 1 to 5; 3 more times, end(RS) right side is last row worked.

Work row 2 one more time, end (WS) wrong side is last row worked.

Change to larger size 8 needles.

Note: A 6 stitch cable is worked the same as a 4 stitch cable, with the exception of placing 3 sts on the cable needle instead of 2, knitting the next 3 sts, then knitting the sts from the cable needle.

Yoke
Row 1 (RS) Inc row and cable row: 1 stitch will be added to each side of every cable to make them 6 st cables on this row only): *P2 (2, 3, 3, 3), P1inc, (purl in front of st and in back of same stitch), 4 st lt cable, p1inc in first p st after cable, * rep bet *'s. end p2 (2, 3, 3, 3). Note: you are increasing in the last and first p st on each side of the cable. Turn.

Row 2: K3 (3, 4, 4, 4), p6; rep around, end k3 (3, 4, 4, 4). Turn. Always work 6 cable sts as established, knit purl increase sts on wrong side and purl them on the right side.

Rows 3, 4, 5, 6: Knit k sts, and purl p sts

Row 7: (Inc row and cable row) * Inc in p st before cable by working a p1inc, twist cable, p1inc in the first p st after cable, purl to st before cable,* repeat across row.

Rows 8, 9, 10, 11, 12: Knit k sts, purl p sts, treat increase sts as purls on right side and knits on wrong side. Repeat this pattern increasing every 6th row on each side of cable until yoke measures: 13 (14, 15, 16, 17)" including neck ribbing.

Sleeves
(RS) Work 3 sts past 2nd cable, change to smaller size 8 16" circular needles or dp needles. Work past 3rd and 4th cable to within 3 sts of 5th cable. Place marker and join sleeve to knit circular. Cont in est pattern of purls and knit cables every 7th row with no increases, at the same time, dec 1 st before and after marker on same row when cable is twisted. When sleeve inseam measures 14 (15, 15, 16, 16)" or desired length, change to smaller size 4 16" needles or dp to work cuff circular.

Cuff

There should be approx 48 to 56 sts, should be divisible by 8. Decreases may need to be made on first round of cuff if too many sts remain.

Rows 1 to 4: K4, p4; rep around lining up the knit sts and purl sts.

Row 5: *4 st right cable, p4 *; rep around.

Rep rows 1 to 5; 4 more times.

Work rows 1 to 4; bind off loosely.

Repeat for other sleeve, attaching yarn after sts are slipped to other sleeve section 3 sts past 2nd cable.

Body

Remaining sts are body. Continue with established pattern of purls and cables for 11 (11, 12, 12, 13)" or desired length. Change to smaller size 4 needles, and work cuff in same pattern as sleeve cuff. Bind off loosely.

Front Button Band

With smaller size 4 needles and on right side of sweater, pick up sts along front edge, pick up 1 st per row. Number of sts should be a multiple of 4. Turn. Work p4, k4, along front edge. Work cables every 4th row. After 8 rows of band are worked, make button holes between every 3 cables on purl sts by binding off 3 sts, then inc 3 sts on next row. Continue to work ribbing until it measures 2", bind off loosely. Repeat button band for left side, with no button holes.

Finishing

With variegated yarn, work a blanket stitch edging along outside edge of sweater, collar, fronts and bottom. Repeat for both sleeve cuffs. Follow embroidery for flower vine and leaves. Embroider vine and leafs in green yarn. Embroider flowers in variegated yarn (see chart), and knots in variegated yarn. Sew on buttons. Buttonholes may need to be reinforced with a blanket stitch using same yarn as was used for sweater. Weave in ends and block.

Finished measurements for sweater

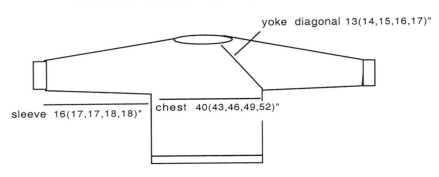

yoke diagonal 13(14,15,16,17)"

sleeve 16(17,17,18,18)"

chest 40(43,46,49,52)"

42

Embroidery layout for front and sleeves

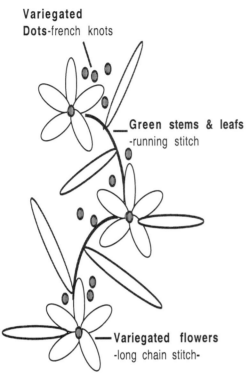

Variegated Dots-french knots

Green stems & leafs -running stitch

Variegated flowers -long chain stitch-

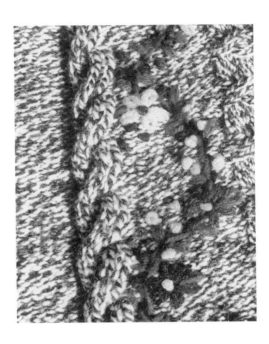

Country Checked Cardigan
No Farming Chores in This

A great cardigan to be worn with jeans or dress up with any ensemble. Knit with worsted weight Shetland Ragg yarn, complimented with blue, gold, green and burgundy for a sweater to match many outfits. Increases are worked into the color chart for a smooth appearance.

Sizes
Sweater is written for sizes; **small, medium, large, x--large, xx--large**. Directions are for smallest size with larger sizes in parenthesis.

Sweater pictured was knit with Paton's Shetland Ragg yarn.

Finished Chest Measurements
Chest circumference 36 (39, 42, 45, 48)"

Materials
Yarn Worsted weight total yards needed: Tan 900 (1000, 1100, 1300, 1500) yds; Blue 450 (500, 550, 600, 650) yds;
1 skein of gold, green and burgundy for contrasting colors.
Circular Needles One pair each size 4 and 8 16"length and size 8 24" length. Size 4 and 8 dp needles can be used instead of 16" circular needles.
Markers
Buttons

Gauge

4 sts and 7 rows = 1" knit with Shetland Ragg Yarn and size 8 needles in Stockinette stitch. Gauge may vary with different yarn.

Neck Ribbing

With size 4 circular needles and blue yarn cast on 106 (110, 114, 118, 122) sts, turn. Begin color chart now. Work k2, p2, ribbing across row, turn. Repeat k2, p2 ribbing back and forth lining up the knit sts and purl sts. Buttonhole will be worked after 1" of ribbing is complete.

Button Bands & Buttonholes

A single crocheted edge was worked along both fronts for bands. 3 rows of single crochet and buttonholes were worked by chaining 2 sts where buttonholes are to be placed.

Note The button bands can be worked in garter stitch, knitting the first and last 5 sts on all rows. Continue making buttonholes down the right band of sweater as often as desired or 3" apart by binding off 2 sts, then casting on 2 sts on next row where sts were bound off.

Preparatory Row: Change to larger size 8 24" needles, (RS) place the following markers: k5, k15 (16, 17, 18, 19), place marker, k18 (19, 20, 20, 21), place marker, k30 (30, 30, 32, 32), place marker, k18 (19, 20, 20, 21), place marker, k15 (16, 17,18, 19), k5, turn.

M1 Make 1 stitch: On knit side, with left needles, pick up the horizontal strand between last st and next st to be knit, pick it up from front to back and knit into the back of this strand with the right needle. Strand is twisted to avoid a hole. See pattern notes for detailed pictures.
Note Knit first and last 5 sts of button bands down both front edges for entire front even though the instructions don't have it written out on each row.
Row 1 and all odd rows: Purl.
Row 2: Knit row and M1 2 sts before and after each marker.

Optional Short Row Explanation and Directions to be worked now. (If you don't want to work short rows, cont with yoke directions) Don't follow color chart for short rows, work them in same color as neck ribbing. 4 optional short rows may be added to the back and part of the sleeve sections of the sweater for a more comfortable fit. Short rows are knit after neck ribbing is finished and you have changed to larger needles. WS, Slip beg marker (1st marker) and purl to the 4th marker. P2 sts past 4th marker, yarn back (yb), sl 1, yarn forward (yf), turn work to (RS), sl 1 st, knit to beg marker, knit 2 sts past beg marker, yf, sl 1, yb, turn work, (WS), sl 1st, purl to where last turn was made (2 sts past the 4th marker) purl 2 sts past last short row turn, yb, sl 1 st, yf, turn work, (RS), sl 1 st, knit to end of row. Continue with row 4.
Row 4: M1 6 sts before and after markers, turn.

Row 6: K row and at same time M1 8 sts before and after markers.

Row 8: Knit row and at same time, M1 2 sts before and after marker.

Row 10 and every even row: You will continue to M1 before and after marker , changing the placement of the M1 on each row. By altering their placement, there will be no raglan line. You can place them farther away from the markers as more sts are added.

Note Make sure you are consistent in their placement and they are the same distance away from each marker for that row. When yoke measures: 11 (12, 13, 14, 15)", end (WS).

Sleeve

Knit to the sleeve section which will be the first marker from the front edge to the 2nd marker, begin using the size 8 16" circular needles, or size 8 dp needles, join to knit circular, place a marker where the two edge of the sleeve joined. Continue knitting circular with the following sleeve inseam decreases.

Rows 1 to 5: Knit

Row 6: K2tog before and after marker while knitting row.

Continue decreasing every 6th row until sleeve is about 7" from where you want the length. Begin working the color chart starting on row 28 and work BACKWARDS to row 1. Change to smaller size 4 dp or size 4 16" circular needles for cuff, cont with color chart to row 1r. Make sure you have a multiple of 4 sts remaining.

Cuff

K2, p2, ribbing for 3" lining up the knit and purl sts. Bind off loosely.

Slip sts over to other sleeve section which is between the 3rd and 4th markers. Attach yarn on first st and repeat same directions for second sleeve using size 8 16" or dp needles.

Body

All remaining sts will be joined for body of sweater. When joining under sleeves and to close the small gap, with left needle, pick up 2 sts from sleeve section and knit them. On next row when you get to those sts added, k2tog twice to decrease the added sts. Continue with body working back and forth until it is 11 (11, 12, 12, 13)" desired length or the length of the sleeve.

Cuff

Change to smaller size 4 needles and work a k2, p2, ribbing for 2". You may need to decrease a few sts to have the ribbing a multiple of 4. Bind off loosely.

Finishing

Weave in yarn ends, sew on buttons and if needed work a small blanket stitch around each buttonhole for reinforcement. Embroider a running chain stitch up the edge of the garter st button band on both sides of the fronts with CC. The outside edge of the sweater can have a single crochet edge worked around it or a blanket stitch with the blue yarn.

Color Key

t	tan
y	yellow
g	green
b	blue
r	red

Finished sweater measurements

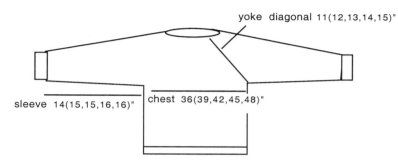

yoke diagonal 11(12,13,14,15)"

sleeve 14(15,15,16,16)"   chest 36(39,42,45,48)"

Color Chart for Country Cardigan The letter "r" refers to ribbing rows.

Begin each row from the right side from row 1 and as more sts are added, line up the colors according to the chart. You may need to adjust the row to line up the colors. Where sts are added, you may be off a little, but it won't show when the yoke is complete. Stop on chart when yoke is size desired.

b	b	b	b	1r	t	t	t	t	9	b	b	b	b	29	t	t	t	t	49	y	y	r	r	69
b	b	b	b	2r	t	t	t	t	10	t	t	t	t	30	t	t	t	t	50	y	y	r	r	70
b	b	b	b	3r	t	t	t	t	11	t	t	t	t	31	t	t	t	t	51	r	r	y	y	71
b	b	b	b	4r	t	t	t	t	12	t	t	t	t	32	t	t	t	t	52	r	r	y	y	72
y	y	y	y	5r	b	b	b	b	13	t	t	t	t	33	r	r	r	r	53	t	t	t	t	73
b	b	b	b	6r	b	b	b	b	14	g	g	g	g	34	r	r	r	r	54	t	t	t	t	74
b	b	b	b	7r	b	b	y	y	15	t	t	t	t	35	r	r	r	r	55	t	t	t	t	75
b	b	b	b	8r	b	b	y	y	16	t	t	t	t	36	y	y	y	y	56	g	g	g	g	76
r	r	r	r	9r	r	r	r	r	17	t	t	t	t	37	y	y	y	y	57	g	g	g	g	77
b	b	b	b	10r	r	r	r	r	18	r	r	r	r	38	y	y	y	y	58	b	b	b	b	78
b	b	b	b	11r	r	r	g	g	19	t	t	t	t	39	y	y	y	y	59	b	b	b	b	79
b	b	b	b	12r	r	r	g	g	20	t	t	t	t	40	y	y	b	b	60	b	b	y	y	80
t	t	t	t	1	y	y	y	y	21	t	t	t	t	41	b	b	b	b	61	b	b	y	y	81
t	t	t	t	2	y	y	y	y	22	t	t	y	y	42	b	b	b	b	62	r	r	r	r	82
t	t	t	t	3	b	b	y	y	23	t	t	y	y	43	b	b	b	b	63	r	r	r	r	83
t	t	t	t	4	b	b	y	y	24	b	b	b	b	44	b	b	b	b	64	r	r	r	r	84
b	b	b	b	5	b	b	b	b	25	b	b	b	b	45	b	b	b	b	65	t	t	g	g	85
b	b	b	b	6	b	b	b	b	26	g	g	t	t	46	b	b	b	b	66	t	t	g	g	86
b	b	b	b	7	b	b	b	b	27	g	g	t	t	47	b	b	b	b	67	t	t	t	t	87
b	b	b	b	8	b	b	b	b	28	t	t	t	t	48	b	b	b	b	68	t	t	t	t	88

Twist 'n Knit
Dance All Night

Dk variegated yarn mixed with a solid creates this pullover knit from the top down, the yarn overs in the yoke will make the increases smooth and flowing. A twist stitch is worked between the lacework to create a zigzag effect. The longer the yoke, the larger the sweater.

Sizes

Sweater is written for sizes; **small, medium, large, x-large and xx-large.** Sweater instructions are written for size small with larger sizes in parenthesis.

Sweater pictured knit with Patons Astra dk yarn.

Finished Chest Measurements
Chest circumference 38 (41, 44, 47, 50)"

Materials
Yarn Sport Weight, two strands held together, one variegated and one plain to match variegated. Total yardage needed of each color: 1100 (1200, 1300, 1500, 1750)yds.
Circular Needles (Ribbing) For sizes S and M one pair each circular size 6 and 8 16" and 24" lengths. For sizes L, XL, XXL one pair each circular size 7 and 10 16" and 24"lengths and
Tapestry Needle
Markers

Gauge

4 sts and 5 to 6 rows = 1 inch knit with double strand sport weight yarn and size 8 needles knit in Stockinette stitch. Gauge may vary with different yarn.
3 to 4 sts knit with size 10 needles.

Abbreviations

K1inc Knit into the front of the stitch and again into the back strand of the same stitch before slipping stitch off left needle.

M1 Make one stitch; With left needle tip, lift the strand between the last knitted stitch and the first stitch on the left needle, from front to back, knit through the front of the lifted strand, this will leave a hole.

SKP Slip 1 stitch knit wise then knit 1 st, pass slipped stitch over.

K2tog Knit 2 stitches together.

Lt tw Left twist ; will slant left, with tip of right needle, go behind first to second st on left needle, place needle through second stitch from top to bottom, wrap yarn around as if to knit, then knit first st on needle normally, drop both sts off left needle at same time

Rt tw Right twist; will slant right, with right needle, knit second stitch first, then first st, by slipping rt needle knit wise, through second stitch, wrap st and bring forward as knit st, don't drop st off, then knit first st and drop both off at the same time.

Note: From before a twist st to after a twist st is one "section". You will count sections later on to divide for sleeves, front and back. Sizes small to XXL are worked to rows 53 (59, 65, 72, 78).

Neck

With size 6 (6, 7, 7, 7) needles, cast on 80 sts. Join to knit circular making sure stitches are not twisted. Place beginning marker.

Row 1: K2, p2; rep around to beginning marker.

Rep row 1 for 2 1/2" .

Change to larger size 8 (8, 10, 10, 10) needles 24" length. Place marker. Knit the following rows and continue for larger sizes.

 Note: Photocopy pattern and check off each row as it is knit to help keep track of place. Repeat instructions between *'s for each row continuously around to beg marker

___**Row 1:** *Rt tw, k1, m1, k1,* Rep around to beg marker.

___**Row2:** *Lt tw, k3,*

___**Row 3:** *Rt tw, k1, yo, skp,*

___**Row 4:** *Lt tw , k3,*

___**Row 5:** *Rt tw, k3,*

___**Row 6:** *Lt tw, yo, k1, k2tog, yo,* (inc row)

___**Row 7:** *Rt tw, k4* (you may have to move marker 1 stitch)

___**Row 8:** *Lt tw, k4,*

___**Row 9:** *Rt tw, yo, k2tog, k2tog, yo,*

___**Row 10:** *Lt tw, k4*, rep.

___**Row 11:** *Rt tw, k1, yo, k1, yo, skp,*

___**Row 12:** *Lt tw, k5,*

___**Row 13:** *Rt tw, k5,*

___**Row 14:** *Rt tw, k2tog, yo, k1inc, yo, skp,* (inc row)

___**Row 15:** *Lt tw, k6,*

___**Row 16:** *Rt tw, k2tog, yo, k2, yo, skp,*

___**Row 17:** *Lt tw, k6,*

___**Row 18:** *Rt tw, k6,*

___**Row 19:** *Lt tw, k2tog, yo, k1, m1, k1, yo, skp,* (inc row)

___**Row 20:** *Rt tw, k7,*

___**Row 21:** *Lt tw, k2tog, yo, k3, yo, skp,*

___**Row 22:** *Rt tw, k7,*.

___**Row 23:** *Lt tw, k7,*.

___**Row 24:** *Rt tw, k2tog, yo, k1,m1, k2, yo, skp,* (inc row)

___**Row 25:** *Lt tw, k8,*

___**Row 26:** *Rt tw, k2tog, yo, k4, yo, skp,*

___**Row 27:** *Lt tw, k8,*

___**Row 28:** *Rt tw, k2tog, yo, k4, yo, skp,*

___**Row 29:** *Lt tw, k8,*

___**Row 30:** *Rt tw, k2,tog, yo,k2, yo, k2, yo, skp,* (inc row)

___**Row 31:** *Lt tw, k9,*

___**Row 32:** *Rt tw, k2tog, yo, k2tog, yo, k1, yo, skp, yo, skp,*

___**Row 33:** *Lt tw, k9,*

___**Row 34:** *Rt tw, k2tog, yo, k2tog, yo, k1, yo, skp, yo, skp,*

___**Row 35:** *Lt tw, k9,*

___**Row 36:** *Rt tw, k2tog, yo, k2tog, yo, k1inc, yo, skp, yo, skp,* (inc row)

___**Row 37:** *Lt tw, k10,*

___**Row 38:** *Rt tw, k2tog, yo, k2tog, yo, k2, yo, skp, yo, skp*

___**Row 39:** *Lt tw, k10,*

___**Row 40:** *Rt tw, k2tog, yo, k2tog, yo, k2, yo, skp, yo, skp,*

___**Row 41:** *Lt tw, k10,*

___**Row 42:** *Rt tw, k2tog, yo, k2tog, yo, k1, yo, k1, yo, skp, yo, skp,* (inc row)

___**Row 43:** *Lt tw, k11,*

___**Row 44:** *Rt tw, k2tog, yo, k2tog, yo, k3, yo, skp, yo, skp,*

___**Row 45:** *Lt tw, k11,*

___**Row 46:** *Rt tw, k2t,og, yo, k2tog, yo, k3, yo, skp, yo, skp,*

___**Row 47:** *Lt tw, k11,*

___**Row 48:** *Rt tw, k2tog, yo, k2tog, yo, k2, yo, k2, yo, skp, yo, skp,* (inc row)

___**Row 49:** *Lt tw, k12,*

___**Row 50:** *Rt tw, k2tog, yo, k2tog, yo,k5, yo, skp, yo, skp,*
___**Row 51:** *Lt tw, k12,*
___**Row 52:** *Rt tw, k2tog, yo, k2tog, yo, k5, yo, skp, yo, skp,*
___**Row 53:** *Lt tw, k12,*

Yoke should measure from base of neck ribbing to end approx 11" and 20 sections of 14 sts, approx 280 sts.

Size Medium:
___**Row 54:** *Rt tw, k2tog, yo, k2tog, yo, k2, k1inc, k2, yo, skp, yo, skp,* (inc row)
___**Row 55:** *Lt tw, k13,*
___**Row 56:** *Rt tw, k2tog, yo, k2tog, yo, k6, yo, skp, yo, skp,*
___**Row 57:** *Lt tw, k13,*
___**Row 58:** *Rt tw, k2tog, yo, k2tog, yo, k6, yo, skp, yo, skp,*
___**Row 59:** *Lt tw, k13,*
Yoke should measure from base of neck ribbing to end approx 12" and 20 sections of 15 sts, approx 300 sts.

Size Large:
___**Row 60:** *Rt tw, k2tog, yo, k2tog, yo, k3, yo, k3, yo, skp, yo, skp,* (inc row)
___**Row 61:** *Lt tw, k14,*
___**Row 62:** *Rt tw, k2tog, yo, k2tog, yo, k7, yo, skp, yo, skp,*
___**Row 63:** *Lt tw, k14,*
___**Row 64:** *Rt tw, k2tog, yo, k2tog, yo, k7, yo, skp, yo, skp,*
___**Row 65:** *Lt tw, k14,*
Yoke should measure from base of neck ribbing to end approx 13" and 20 sections of 16 sts, approx 320 sts.

Size X-Large:
___**Row 66:** *Rt tw, k2tog, yo, k2tog, yo, k3, k1inc, k3, yo, skp, yo, skp,* (inc row)
___**Row 68:** *Lt tw, k15,*
___**Row 69:** *Rt tw, k2tog, yo, k2tog, yo, k8, yo, skp, yo, skp,*
___**Row 70:** *Lt tw, k15,*
___**Row 71:** *Rt tw, k2tog, yo, k2tog, yo, k8, yo, skp, yo, skp*.
___**Row 72:** *Lt tw, k15*.
Yoke should measure from base of neck ribbing to underarm approx 14" and 20 sections of 17 sts, approx 340 sts.

Size XX-Large:
___**Row 73:** *Rt tw, k2tog, yo, k2tog, yo, k4, yo, k4, yo, skp, yo, skp,* (inc row)
___**Row 74:** *Lt tw, k16,*

___**Row 75:** *Rt tw, k2tog, yo, k2tog, yo, k9, yo, skp, yo, skp,*
___**Row 76:** *Lt tw, k16,*
___**Row 77:** *Rt tw, k2tog, yo, k2tog, yo, k9, yo, k3, yo, skp, yo, skp,*
___**Row 78:** *Lt tw, k16,*

Yoke should measure from base of neck ribbing to end approx 15"and 20 sections of 18 sts, approx 360 sts.

Sleeve

Keeping all other sts on needles, use the 16" length size 8 (8, 10, 10, 10) needles and knit over the following sleeve section which starts at the beg marker which should be in front of twist st. Work established pattern over 70 (75, 80, 85, 90) sts. Join these stitches and place marker which will be the sleeve inseam. Knit sleeve circular continuing pattern for sleeve by repeating the last 2 rows that were knit for yoke which should be a combination of twist sts, yo's, k2tog's and knit sts and a row of twist sts and knit sts. Decrease two sts by k2tog every 6th row before and after marker, or not working the yo's closest to the markers if they are close to the sleeve inseam. Knit sleeve until inseam measures 13 (14, 14, 15, 15)". Make sure you have remaining sts a multiple of 4.

Cuff

Change to size 6 (6, 7, 7, 7) circular needles and work; k2, p2, ribbing for 3".
Slip sts over 5 sections and repeat for other sleeve, make sure front and back match in number of sts.

Body

All remaining sts are body of sweater. Attach yarn and join front and back to knit body circular. Continue working last two rows of yoke pattern. Knit body in established pattern until it measures the desired length, or the length of body from armhole; 9 (10, 10, 11, 12)".

Note: There will be a small hole under each sleeve where front and back are joined. This gap can be knit closed or sewn later after sweater is completed.

Body Ribbing

Change to smaller size 6 (6, 7, 7, 7) needles and work k2, p2 ribbing for 2 to 3". Bind off loosely

Finishing

Weave in tail ends and spray with water mist and press with palms of hands to block.

Finished sweater measurements

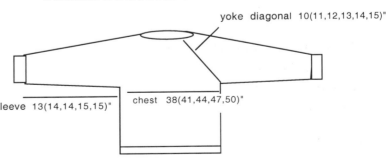

yoke diagonal 10(11,12,13,14,15)"

sleeve 13(14,14,15,15)"

chest 38(41,44,47,50)"

52

Shades of Gray
Soft and Smooth

Mixed shades of gray, blend together for a subtle fair isle yoke sweater. Knit in the traditional raglan style from the top down, choose colors that compliment each other and knit away. Make another sweater and change the color chart and create a matching sweater.

Sizes
Sizes can be adjusted to fit either ladies or men. Sweater is written for sizes; **small**, **medium**, **large**, **x-large and xx-large.** Directions are written for smallest size with larger sizes in parenthesis.

Sweater pictured is knit with Paton's Canadiana Yarn.

Finished Chest Measurements
Chest circumference 36 (39, 42, 45, 48)"

Materials
Yarn worsted weight total yardage for Main color: 950 (1050, 1150, 1350, 1550). 1 skein of 2 other shades to match main color.
Circular Needles One pair each size 4 and 8 16" length, Size 4 and 8 24" length .
Markers
Tapestry Needle

Gauge

4 to 5 sts and 6 to 7 rows = 1" knit with worsted weight yarn in Stockinette st and size 8 needles. Gauge will vary with different yarn.

Neck Edge

With size 4 circular needles, cast on 88 (92, 96, 100, 104, 108) stitches. **Note**: If bulkier yarn is used, larger needles may be substituted to allow for larger yarn.

Row 1: K1, p1; repeat across row. (do not turn)

Row 2: Place beginning marker on right needle, join beginning of row with end of row to begin circular knitting, make sure stitches are not twisted. Continue with k1, p1, ribbing lining up the knit and purl stitches for the rib pattern slipping markers as you knit around until neck ribbing measures 3 to 4" and will later be folded over and stitched. End work at beg marker.

Preparation Row: Change to larger size 8 needles and slip marker to larger needles, *K1 increase. (knit in the front of the stitch, and back of same stitch to increase 1 stitch.) K14 (15, 16, 17, 18, 19) k1 inc, place marker, k1 inc, k26, (27, 28, 29, 30, 31), k1 inc, place marker, * rep bet *'s once. Sweater is now divided into front, back and sleeves.

Optional short rows explanation (If you don't want to work short rows, continue with yoke directions below.) Four optional short rows are explained here and may be knit after neck ribbing is finished and you have changed to larger needles. (RS) Slip beginning marker (1st marker) and knit to the 4th marker. K2 sts past 4th marker, yarn forward (yf), sl 1, yarn back (yb), turn work to(WS), sl 1 st, purl to beginning marker, purl 2 sts past beginning marker, yb, sl 1, yf, turn work, (RS), sl 1st, knit to where last turn was made (2 sts past the 4th marker) knit 2 sts past last short row turn, yf, sl 1 st, yb, turn work, (WS) sl 1 st, purl to beg marker, purl 4 sts past beg marker. yb, sl 1, yf, turn work, (RS) sl 1 st, knit to beg marker. You have just added 4 rows to the back and part of the sleeve sections of the sweater for a more comfortable fit.

Note: Begin color chart and start each row from beg marker and slip markers as you go.

Row 1: Knit row.

Row 2: Knit row increasing 1 stitch before and after each marker.

Repeat rows 1 and 2 until yoke measures 11 (12, 13, 14, 15, 16) " ribbing not included. (Measure along raglan seam line.)

Note: The sleeve sections are narrower than front and back. Sleeves are worked first, keeping all other stitches on needle.

Sleeve

With shorter 16" size 8 needles, slip beginning marker and knit to the 2nd marker (sleeve section). Join beginning to end of sleeve section to knit circular. Place marker when joining stitches to mark inseam.

Rows 1 to 5 : Knit .

Row 6: Knit 2tog after slipping marker, work to last two stitches and k2tog before marker. Rep rows 1 to 6 until sleeve inseam measures 15 (15, 16, 16, 17, 17)". End by working rows 3 to 5 for cuff pattern. Make sure you have an even number of sts. You may need to decrease sts.

Cuff

Change to smaller size 4 needles, work in rib stitch k1, p1 for 2 to 3". Bind off loosely
Slip stitches on needle over to other sleeve marker. Attach yarn and repeat sleeve pattern.

Body

All stitches remaining on needles are the lower sweater body. Attach yarn on first stitch and join front and back. When joining, pick up 2 sts from the sleeve inseam to help close the gap in the underarm. On the next round, k2tog 2 times to decrease these added sts. Continue to knit circular until body length is desired length or matches sleeve length, not including ribbing.

Body Cuff

With smaller size 4 needles work k1, p1, ribbing for 2 1/2 to 3". Bind off loosely.

Finishing

Weave tail ends from bottom of sweater and neck edge. Very loosely, fold neck ribbing in half toward the inside and stitch in place. Block with water and spray mist and press with hand.

Finished sweater measurements

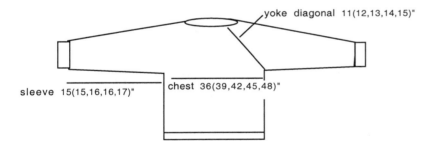

yoke diagonal 11(12,13,14,15)"

sleeve 15(15,16,16,17)"

chest 36(39,42,45,48)"

Color Chart Key

	white
L	Lt gray
D	Dk gray main color

Color chart for Shades of Gray Sweater Pattern

Start with row 1 and always start each row from the right and work to the left side of the chart.

C1	C2	C3	C4	#	C1	C2	C3	C4	#	C1	C2	C3	C4	#	C1	C2	C3	C4	#
D	D	D	D	1	L	L		L	16	D	D	D	D	31	L	L	L	L	46
D	D	D	D	2	L	L	L	L	17	D		D		32			D	D	47
D	L	D	L	3	L	L	L	L	18	D		D		33			D	D	48
L	L	L	L	4	L	L	L	L	19					34	D	D	D	D	49
L	L	L	L	5		D	D	D	20	L	L	L	L	35	L	L	L	L	50
D	D	D		6		D	D	D	21	L	D	L	D	36	L	L	L	L	51
	D			7	D	D	D	D	22	L	L	L	L	37		D		D	52
				8		D			23	D	D	D	D	38		L		L	53
L				9	D		D		24	D	D	D	D	39		D		D	54
L	L	L	L	10					25	D	D		D	40					55
L	D	L	D	11					26	D				41					56
D	L	D	L	12			L	L	27					42	L		L		57
D	D	D	D	13			L	L	28		L		L	43	L	D	L	D	58
L	L		L	14	D	D	D	D	29	L	L	L	L	44	D	D	D	D	59
L				15	L	D	L	D	30	D	L	D	L	45	D		D		60

Design Challenge

Create your own memory sweater. The sweater pictured was knit for my father with his hobbies and interests as the topic for motifs. I graphed on paper a small picture of what he liked, then colored it on graph paper. I tried to limit the colors used at one time to 2 or 3 colors. For some of the motifs, I alternated them upside down, right side up for a unique look. I worked the increases every other row in between the designs. If you look closely, you can see his name, and many of his hobbies which include, music, saxophone, ceramics, medicine, pottery, bowling, fish and it buttoned with coin buttons. Lots of fun and really not too hard, just exciting to see the sweater come to life.

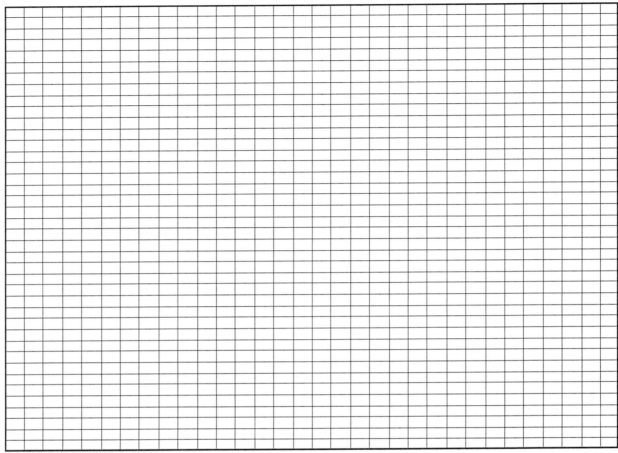

Design Away....Chart your own motifs.

Suggested Yarn Sources

Heindselmans Knit Shop
176 West Center Street
Provo, Utah
801-373-5193 fax 801 373-9664

The Knitting room
3189 Meridian Ave
San Jose CA 95124
408 264-7229
Knitroom@aol.com

Lion Brand Yarn CO
34 West 15 Street
New York, NY 10011
800-258-9276

www.the-mannings.com

www.wanderings.com

Needles'n Pins Yarn Shoppe
W9034 County Trunk A
Delavan WI 53115
www.needlespinsyarnshoppe.com

Patternworks Yarn Warehouse
Poughkeepsie, NY
1-800-438-5464
www.patternworks.com
knit@patternworks.com

Plymouth Yarn Co., Inc
P.O. Box 28
Bristol, PA 19007
http://www.plymouthyarn.com

Unique One
P.O. Box 744
Camden ME 04843
www.mainesweaters.com

**Wanderknits-Country Store & Mail
   Order**
1944 Washington Valley Rd.
Martinsville, NJ 08836
800 456-knit www.elan.com

Weaver's Loft
Yarnshop@aol.com
800 693-7243

YarnXpress
www.YarnXpress.com
info@yarnxpress.com
23 Compass Avenue
West Milford, NY 07480

Stitch Glossary

Approx: An abbreviation for the word approximately.

Bind off (bo) Decreasing stitches at end of work to finish off edge.

Cast on (co) Adding stitches to the needles to knit.

Contrasting color (cc) Colors in the work that are used less than the others.

Chain (ch) An abbreviation for a crocheted chain stitch made by making a loop and drawing the yarn through the loop with the crochet hook.

Color Chart Chart that is followed for color changes in garment. Start chart from the bottom right side on row 1 and start each row from the right side unless otherwise noted.

Continue (cont) Keep working as you have been.

Decrease (dec) A process to take away sts so there are fewer than originally.

Double Point (dp) Needles that are pointed on both ends, used to knit circular.

Duplicate stitch An embroidery stitch worked on top of the knitting, woven to look like a knit stitch.

Established (est) An abbreviation for established.

Fair Isle A combination of different colors worked together in a design, usually.

Garter Stitch A type of knitting in which the knit stitch is worked on both sides, leaving a ridge for each row.

Gauge The number of stitches and row in a knitted sample.

Increase (inc) You will increase a stitch either by M1 or K1inc where indicated in pattern.

Garter Stitch Both sides of the work are knit. Knit on the knit side of the work and knit on

the purl side also.

Knit (k) Abbreviation for knit.

Knit in front and back A method of increasing one stitch by knitting into the front of the stitch and before dropping it off the needle, knitting into the back of the same stitch.

Knit Two Sitiches Together (K2tog) Knit 2 stitches together. Place needle through second and first stitch at the same time, follow through

with the knit stitch.

Knit One Stitch and Increase (K1inc) Knit into the front of the stitch and into knit normally and before slipping stitch off needle, knit again into the back strand of the same stitch, then slip stitch off left needle.

Knitwise Insert the needle front to back as if to knit.

Left Cable (lt cable) Placing sts on a cable needle and holding to the front of the work, the next sts are worked, then the sts from the cable needle are worked for a twisted appearance.

Left Twist (Lt tw) = Left twist will slant left, With tip of right needle, go behind first and second st on left needle, bring needle between purl wise, wrap front of 2nd st from top to bottom around right needle and pull through to back wrap yarn and bring st forward knit wise, then, knit first st on left needle, drop both sts off left needle at same time

Marker (m) A small ring or other item used to mark place on needle.

Main Color (mc) The color of yarn used most in the knitting.

Make One Stitch (M1) With left needle tip,

lift the strand between the last knitted stitch and the first stitch on the left needle, from front to back, knit through the back of the lifted strand, this will not leave a hole.

Multiple The number of stitches that make up a sequence of stitches that are in a pattern.

Parenthesis Curved vertical lines that contain directions that will be repeated.

Pass Slipped Stitch Over (psso) After slipping a stitch from the left needle to the right, the instructions may have "psso". You work the next stitch after slipping a stitch, then slip the left needle through the slipped stitch and lift it over the last stitch worked. This will decrease 1 stitch.

Picot A series of bumps along a knitted edge.

Purl (p) Work the next stitch a purl. Slip the needle from back to front and from the top down.

Purlwise Insert the needle from the back to the front as you would to purl.

Raglan sleeve A type of sleeve that tapers from the neck down to the arm on a diagonal.

repeat (rep) Means to do something over again.

Ribbing A name for fabric that is worked in such a way that gives it elasticity, usually a combination on knit and purl stitches.

Round In circular knitting, each row is sometimes called a round.

Right Hand (rh) Reference to right hand, stitches or needle.

Right Side(RS) Refers to the right side of the work.

Right Cable (rt cable) Placing sts on a cable needle and holding to the back of the work, the next sts are worked, then the sts from the cable needle are worked for a twisted appearance.

Right Twist (rt tw) Right twist will slant right, with right needle, knit second stitch first, then first st, by slipping rt needle knit wise, through second stitch, wrap st and bring forward as knit st, don't drop st off, then knit first st and drop both off at the same time.

Short row A way of turning part way through a row and working back and forth over stitches to create extra rows for a more comfortable shaping,.

Slip, Knit, Pass Slipped Stitch over Knit Stitch (skp) Slip one stitch from left needle to right needle, work the next stitch, then pass slipped stitch over the kit stitch.

Slip stitch (sl 1) Slip a stitch from the left needle to the right needle. Place the right needle through the loop on the left needle as if you were purling. Slip it over to the other needle without working it. Slip stitch is done.

Slip Marker (sm) Slip marker from the left needle to the right needle.

Stockinette Stitch (St st) If knitting circular, you will knit all rows circular. If working two sided, you will knit the right side and purl the wrong side.

Through Back Loop (tbl) Instead of knitting into the front of the stitch, place needle through the back loop instead and work the stitch as usual.

Work Refers to the project you are working on.

WS Abbreviation for the wrong side.

Yarn Back (yb) Place throw yarn to the back of the work as if to knit.

Yarn Forward (yf) Place throw yarn to the front of the work as if to purl.

Yarn Over (yo) Place throw yarn to the opposite direction, up and over work to the other side.

Yards (yds) Measurement of yarn.

TEACHING KNITTING TO THOSE WHO WATCH

I recently came to the realization that I am not alone with my knitting obsession. All these years I thought I was alone. Until recently, I haven't realized how many people watch me knit or how many I have influenced. Their comments have rolled off my shoulders such as; "I wish I could do that." or "I could never knit." My new comeback has been, "Well, let me teach you." To my surprise, they enthusiastically agree. What is more, they are really knitting and loving it. I am finding delight in teaching others.

I'll admit, I am an obsessive knitter hauling my bag with me wherever I go. It's my emotional security blanket, calming my nerves, relaxing me and boosting my self confidence with each new accomplishment. I seem to handle life's altercations when I'm able to take it out on my knitting. Perhaps it's because I'm sharing my frustrations with my handiwork.

My husband is an incredible man who realized when we were married, he would share me with my hobbies. My hands keep busy while watching television, during football games, while talking on the phone or riding in the car. I don't drive and knit, although I have been tempted. It's amazing how much is accomplished during those moments waiting for children to finish dance lessons, or sit through gymnastic lessons. My hands knit row upon row until my project takes shape.

Do you wonder what you do all day or what you have accomplished? It is the small time fillers that eat up the day, yet time that could be used constructively if two things were done concurrently. Most of my knitting takes place in five or ten minute segments. "Mom, will you teach me how to do that?" asked my nine-year-old daughter McKenzie. I wondered if she was old enough to learn how to knit. We sat together and I mustered up all my patience to begin this trying task. To my surprise, she picked it up very quickly and was soon knitting away.

McKenzie began to knit while watching television riding in the car, and even during school recess. It was time to teach her the art of knitting a sweater. I began teaching her my one piece, top down sweater that anyone can make if they can knit and purl. She chose the yarn and began. "Is this it?" McKenzie asked, as her sweater began to take shape. A few days later, she asked if I would teach a few of her friends how to knit. They had watched her knit and wanted to learn. Soon, there were ten neighborhood girls gathered. With supplies in hand, we taught each of them how to knit. Some were a little shaky, but since we lived close, they were welcome to come over for help. Her friendship with the girls grew closer as they knit together. I didn't expect them to all enjoy knitting, but to my surprise, all did but two girls. Our neighborhood knitting girls meet every couple of weeks to learn a new stitch, or just gather to chat. The excitement spreads as they learn more or just sit and chat while they knit.

Working with the hands while listening can actually increase comprehension. A human brain has two sides, a right and a left. The left brain function is analytical dealing with such activities as listening, reading, math and talking. The right brain deals with creativity, looking at lines and shapes, music and melody. Knitting is a right brain creative activity. The brain automatically shifts from left function to right during a day's activity. While doing something such knitting and listening, both sides of the brain can be in use at the same time, as capacity increases greatly and comprehension heightens. Dr. Betty Edwards, a professor at the California State University has written in her book "Drawing on the Right Side of the Brain," "We have learned that the two hemispheres can work together in many ways." The brain is a phenomenon and knitting can be done along with listening.

My six children never question my constant handiwork. My life is definitely busy. I recently completed a second Master's degree while teaching junior high school full time. Our family of eight takes their share of my time between cooking, cleaning, extracurricular activities, and don't forget that mountain of laundry that never seems to end. In spite of all these daily duties, I still keep those needles clicking, while handling life's dilemmas. Most of my knitting is for my children, which brings great joy to me when they proudly wear the sweater they watched "mom" make just for them.

Faculty meetings are usually a laborious duty, but time passes quickly while knitting during them. After all, the brain is in full use, comprehending while the hands are producing. Several teachers have asked me to teach them to knit. I'm always delighted to share the skill. Now, I'm not the only one knitting at school, there are three of us who knit, two others joined with their crocheting and some bring their cross-stitching. Other teachers watch with interest as they sit empty handed.

An English teacher at my school expressed relief as she told us of her previous inner turmoil while sitting through faculty meetings. The result was a weekly migraine headache. Now that she brings her handiwork, the headaches have disappeared and she leaves the meetings relaxed and ready for the day. Knitting as therapy, what a happy thought. Others watch while the needles are knitting and what is more, it can be learned and enjoyed at any age. There may be others in your own family or at your work watching, waiting to be taught. Take those needles and yarn, a little initiative, and teach others.

Keep those needles knitting.

Mary

Index

About Mary Rich Goodwin

Knitting became Mary's passion at age eight when her grandmother taught her to knit. By age twelve, she was knitting sweaters for family and friends. Her oldest sister, a beautiful knitter born with only one arm and with two small fingers on her right shoulder, taught her new techniques and encouraged her. Her oldest brother, during the VietNam War, learned to knit warm sweaters for himself and others while stationed at a post where he had months of solitude. Her parents, both artists, encouraged her to develop artistic talent in whatever area she worked. They always found the good in her work and a compliment was always waiting.

Mary obtained her teaching degree in Health Education in 1980 from BYU, a Masters Degree in Education in 1988 from Weber State University, and a Masters Degree in Educational Leadership in 1994 from BYU. She has taught Junior High for 19 years, and has written curriculum for her school district. She married in 1980.

Her six children, including five boys and one girl, have been the inspiration for many of her designs. When they were young, money was tight and knitting sweaters was not only fun, but economical. Mary explains that her life has been extremely busy and hectic and she firmly believes that knitting is an excellent form of therapy since it engages one's hands and produces an outcome that brings great satisfaction to oneself and to others.

She is also an advocate for and has participated in humanitarian efforts throughout the world. As a result of donated knitting projects, leapers have comfortable knitted and crocheted bandages, premature babies have caps, and many babies have afghans and booties. Mary encourages others to become involved, saying that there is nothing more satisfying than to give a nice handmade gift to someone and know that you are giving it from your heart.

Mary welcomes comments from her readers and fellow knitters. She encourages people to submit their own designs to knitting magazines.